SpringerBriefs in Law

More information about this series at http://www.springer.com/series/10164

Stephen Barkoczy • Tamara Wilkinson

Incentivising Angels

A Comparative Framework of Tax Incentives for Start-Up Investors

Springer

Stephen Barkoczy
Monash University
Clayton, VIC, Australia

Tamara Wilkinson
Monash University
Clayton, VIC, Australia

ISSN 2192-855X ISSN 2192-8568 (electronic)
SpringerBriefs in Law
ISBN 978-981-13-6631-4 ISBN 978-981-13-6632-1 (eBook)
https://doi.org/10.1007/978-981-13-6632-1

Library of Congress Control Number: 2019933326

This Springer imprint is published by the registered company Springer Nature Singapore Pte Ltd.
The registered company address is: 152 Beach Road, #21-01/04 Gateway East, Singapore 189721, Singapore

Acknowledgements

We wish to thank the Australian Research Council for generously supporting the research for this book under its Discovery Grant scheme (DP130104343) for the project titled 'Designing World-Class Venture Capital Programs to Support the Commercialisation of Australian Research During and Beyond an Economic Crisis'. We also wish to thank four of our Monash law students (Radomir Jovanovic, Benjamin Mescher, Lucy O'Sullivan and Courtney White) who helped with footnoting, proofreading and various other research tasks.

Contents

About the Authors

Stephen Barkoczy BA, LLB, M Tax Law, PhD (Monash University)
Stephen is a Professor in the Faculty of Law at Monash University and a Member of the International Faculty of the Institute for Austrian and International Tax Law at the Vienna University of Economics and Business. Stephen has lectured, researched and practised widely in the areas of taxation, superannuation and venture capital law. He has served on several government and professional committees and currently holds an appointment on the Innovation and Investment Committee of Innovation and Science Australia. Stephen is the author/co-author of many books and the recipient of numerous teaching awards, including the Prime Minister's Award for Australian University Teacher of the Year.

Tamara Wilkinson BA, LLB (Hons) (Monash University)
Tamara has researched in the area of venture capital law for over 6 years and is a co-author of *Innovation and Venture Capital Law and Policy* (Federation Press, 2016). She has taught the subject Private Investment Law alongside Stephen Barkoczy at the masters and undergraduate levels since 2016. Tamara is currently writing her PhD on the topic of government venture capital incentives.

Abbreviations

ATO	Australian Taxation Office
CGT	Capital gains tax
ESI	Early stage investors
ESIC	Early stage innovation company
ESVCLP	Early Stage Venture Capital Limited Partnership
GERD	Gross expenditure on research and development
HMRC	Her Majesty's Revenue and Customs
IPO	Initial public offering
ISA	Innovation and Science Australia
ITA 2007 (UK)	*Income Tax Act 2007* (UK)
ITAA 1997	*Income Tax Assessment Act 1997* (Cth)
MBO	Management buyout
MIC	Management Investment Company
NISA	National Innovation and Science Agenda
OECD	Organisation for Economic Co-operation and Development
PDF	Pooled Development Fund
R&D	Research and development
SEIS	Seed Enterprise Investment Scheme
TAA	*Tax Administration Act 1953* (Cth)
VCLP	Venture Capital Limited Partnership

Chapter 1
Establishing a Comparative Framework of Tax Incentives for Start-Up Investors

Abstract Innovation is critical for economic growth and provides a broad range of spillover benefits for businesses and the broader community. It is therefore not surprising that many governments around the world have been actively involved in formulating polices to stimulate their innovation systems. Governments have focused their attention on a broad range of initiatives, including those specifically targeted at assisting entrepreneurial start-up companies. Start-ups are a key part of a country's innovation system as they are the source of many new business ideas, products and services. One of the problems with start-ups, however, is that they often struggle to access funding from conventional sources, such as banks, and must therefore rely heavily on venture capital investment to grow their businesses. The reality is that without venture capital investment, many start-ups will languish or fail. In order to stimulate venture capital activity in Australia, the Commonwealth Government, as part of its National Innovation and Science Agenda, recently introduced the Early Stage Investors (ESI) program. The ESI program provides generous tax incentives to angel investors who invest in 'early stage innovation companies'. The ESI program is loosely modelled on the United Kingdom's Seed Enterprise Investment Scheme (SEIS) and sits alongside a number of other Australian venture capital tax incentive programs that have been designed to encourage investment in start-ups through specially regulated venture capital funds. This book examines the ESI program and compares and contrasts it with both the United Kingdom's SEIS and Australia's other venture capital tax incentive programs. It critically analyses the programs and draws on the comparative analysis to suggest some ways that the ESI program might be reformed to improve the delivery of its policy objectives.

S. Barkoczy, T. Wilkinson, *Incentivising Angels*, SpringerBriefs in Law,
https://doi.org/10.1007/978-981-13-6632-1_1

1.1 Introduction

Innovation policy has become a central focus of many governments around the world.[1] This is no doubt due to the fact that innovation is widely recognised as an important catalyst for economic growth and prosperity.[2] Entrepreneurial start-up companies, particularly those involved in scientific and technological fields of endeavour, play a key role in a country's innovation system.[3] Start-ups are the source of many new business ideas and are important engines for job creation.[4] They are often involved in undertaking pioneering research initiatives, developing revolutionary products and technologies, and establishing new and untapped markets, which many larger companies may have missed or ignored.[5] The problem with start-ups, however, is that they are extremely risky, and therefore frequently struggle to raise the finance required to carry out their business plans. As a result, it is not surprising that many start-ups languish or fail. Banks are generally reluctant to lend to start-ups because of their small size, lack of track record and the fact that they do not yet have the regular cash-flows necessary to service their loans. In addition, the entrepreneurs who found such companies often do not have the requisite collateral to secure bank loans,[6] and therefore generally have to resort to 'bootstrapping'[7] and contributions from their family and friends to finance their activities. However, as

---

[1] OECD, *Innovation and Growth: Rationale for an Innovation Strategy* (Report, 2007) 3; Jakob Edler and Jan Fagerberg, 'Innovation Policy: What, Why and How' (2017) 33(1) *Oxford Review of Economic Policy* 2.

[2] Australian Government, *National Innovation and Science Agenda–Welcome to the Ideas Boom* (Report, November 2015) 3 ('*National Innovation and Science Agenda*'); Australian Government, *Industry Innovation and Competitiveness Agenda–An Action Plan for a Stronger Australia* (Report, 2014) v; Stephen Barkoczy, Tamara Wilkinson, Ann Monotti and Mark Davison, *Innovation and Venture Capital Law and Policy* (Federation Press, 2016) 18–28; Josh Lerner, *Boulevard of Broken Dreams: Why Public Efforts to Boost Entrepreneurship and Venture Capital Have Failed – and What to Do About It* (Princeton University Press, 2009) 43–5; Directorate-General for Research and Innovation, *State of the Innovation Union 2015* (European Commission Report, 2015) 5; Australian Government, Department of Industry, Innovation and Science, Office of the Chief Economist, *Australian Innovation System Report 2017* (Report, 2017) 6.

[3] John-Christopher Spender, Vincenzo Corvello, Michele Grimaldi and Pierluigi Rippa, 'Startups and Open Innovation: A Review of the Literature' (2017) 20(1) *European Journal of Innovation Management* 4.

[4] Ryan Decker, John Haltiwanger, Ron Jarmin and Javier Miranda, 'The Role of Entrepreneurship in US Job Creation and Economic Dynamism' (2014) 28(3) *Journal of Economic Perspectives* 3, 3–4; StartupAUS, *Crossroads – An Action Plan to Develop a Vibrant Tech Startup Ecosystem in Australia* (Report, 2016) 50; StartupAUS, *Crossroads: An Action Plan to Develop a World-Leading Tech Startup Ecosystem in Australia* (Report, 2017) 22–3.

[5] Stephen Barkoczy and Daniel Sandler, *Government Venture Capital Incentives: A Multi-Jurisdiction Comparative Analysis* (Australian Tax Research Foundation, 2007) 19.

[6] OECD, *Financing High-Growth Firms – The Role of Angel Investors* (OECD, 2011) 19 ('*Financing High Growth Firms*').

[7] Bootstrapping is a term used to refer to situations where entrepreneurs rely on their personal resources to finance their businesses: see further Barkoczy et al. (n 2) 58.

these resources are usually quite limited, the only realistic option for many start-ups to grow their businesses is to raise venture capital from third party investors.

1.2 Venture Capital

Venture capital is a special class of private equity investment.[8] At the most basic level, it involves investors subscribing for shares in small, early stage, unlisted companies with high-growth potential.[9] Venture capital is traditionally divided into two main categories: 'informal venture capital' and 'formal venture capital'.[10] Informal venture capital comes from 'angel investors' who are typically wealthy individuals that have substantial business and entrepreneurial experience.[11] Formal venture capital, on the other hand, comes from 'venture capitalists' who are professional fund managers that have established venture capital funds on behalf of a pool of investors from whom they have raised capital. To help grow their investments and maximise their potential returns, many angels and venture capitalists not only provide finance to start-ups but also use their industry experience and networks to provide them with valuable mentoring support and strategic guidance. This added personal involvement can take up a considerable amount of an investor's time, but is often invaluable to a start-up's founders, particularly those establishing businesses for the first time, as it can help focus the direction of their companies and accelerate their growth trajectories.

The main issue with venture capital is that it is a scarce resource that can be challenging to obtain even in good economic times. This is due to a variety of factors, including the inherent risky nature of this kind of investment and the fact that it can be difficult for investors to realise returns. Angels and venture capitalists typically

---

[8] Venture capital has been described as 'a subset of a larger private equity asset class which includes expansion or growth capital and buyouts': *Financing High Growth Firms* (n 6) 23. Private equity has been described as 'any equity investment in a company that is not publicly traded': Beat A Brechbühl and Bob Wooder, 'General Report' in Beat A Brechbühl and Bob Wooder (eds), *Global Venture Capital Transactions: A Practical Approach* (Kluwer Law International, 2004) 4.

[9] There are many different definitions of venture capital in the literature. The Australian Government, for example, defines venture capital as a 'mechanism for financing new, innovative companies at the pre-seed, seed, start-up and early-expansion stages of commercialisation': Treasury and Department of Industry, Innovation, Science, Research and Tertiary Education, *Review of Venture Capital and Entrepreneurial Skills* (Final Report, 2012) 13. Although venture capital predominantly involves equity investment, it can also sometimes include portions of debt and hybrid investment (e.g., investment using convertible notes).

[10] See further, William Scheela, Edmundo Isidro, Thawatchai Jittrapanun and Nguyen Thi Thu Trang, 'Formal and Informal Venture Capital Investing in Emerging Economies in Southeast Asia' (2015) 32(3) *Asia Pacific Journal of Management* 597; Vanessa Diaz-Moriana and Colm O'Gorman, 'Informal Investors and the Informal Venture Capital Market in Ireland' (2013) 3(6) *Journal of Asian Scientific Research* 630, 632.

[11] *Financing High Growth Firms* (n 6) 21.

have to wait until they exit their investments to make any profits, and it can often take them many years to find buyers for their shares. Venture capital investors therefore need to have a high risk tolerance and a long-term investment horizon. To be successful, they also need to have special skills in locating, evaluating, nurturing and exiting investments.

The reality is that many countries have immature venture capital markets and therefore do not have a sufficiently developed pool of angels and venture capitalists to cater for the financing needs of their start-ups. Formal venture capital, in particular, is often only available to companies that have reached the early-expansion stage of their life cycle. As a consequence, a large portion of start-ups, particularly those at the seed and pre-commercialisation stages of development, must look principally to angels for their initial capital injections.[12] In practice, many start-ups miss out on funding completely, while others may take years to find angels who are willing to back them. The result of this is that many promising innovations do not get developed, or take much longer to commercialise than would otherwise be the case. This can have a negative impact on the levels of entrepreneurship within a country and can stall economic growth and productivity.

1.3 Early Stage Investor Program

In order to support innovation and the development of their countries' start-up sectors, many governments around the world have implemented a broad range of programs to promote venture capital investment.[13] A significant number of these programs rely on tax incentives as the chief mechanism for encouraging venture capital activity to take place.[14]

[12] It has been noted that fewer venture capitalists are investing at the early stages of a start-up's growth and this funding gap has been filled by angel investors who sometimes invest through groups and syndicates: ibid.

[13] These programs are often supplemented by a broad range of other programs that are designed to support start-ups. These other programs include a variety of different kinds of grant, loan, guarantee, incubator, and business assistance programs: see further Barkoczy et al. (n 2) 121–34. Start-ups that have received support under these programs are often more attractive to venture capital investors as they have demonstrated that they can meet the requisite criteria for securing government assistance and have usually benefited from such assistance.

[14] The European Commission has noted that 'tax incentives form part of a broader set of policy tools available to policy makers wishing to incentivise greater levels of business angel and venture capital investment in SMEs and start-ups': European Commission, 'Effectiveness of Tax Incentives for Venture Capital and Business Angels to Foster the Investment of SMEs and Start-ups: Final Report' (Working Paper No 68, European Commission, June 2017) 48. Some of the countries that provide tax incentives to entities that invest in start-ups include Belgium (Tax Shelter for Start-ups and Scale-ups), Canada (Labor-Sponsored Venture Capital Corporations), France (Sociétés de Capital Risque), Germany (INVEST Venture Capital Grant), Ireland (Employment and Investment Incentive), Israel (Angels Law), Italy (Tax Incentives for Investments in Innovative Startups and SMEs), Japan (Tax Incentives to Promote Venture Investment), Malta (Seed Investment Scheme),

To stimulate angel investment in Australia, the Commonwealth Government introduced the Early Stage Investors ('ESI') program on 1 July 2016. The ESI program was announced in December 2015 as part of the Turnbull Government's landmark National Innovation and Science Agenda ('NISA').[15]NISA contained a broad range of measures to support Australia's innovation system and was the first major policy initiative announced by Malcolm Turnbull after he replaced Tony Abbott as Prime Minister.[16] Prior to the announcement of NISA, Australia had been criticised for having one of the world's lowest rates of venture capital investment and for failing to keep pace with many other countries that had launched programs to support start-ups.[17] In NISA, the Government acknowledged that many Australian start-ups have insufficient access to early stage capital, and recognised that this was an impediment to the country becoming a leading innovator.[18] The ESI program seeks to address this problem by providing generous tax incentives to investors who subscribe for shares in 'early stage innovation companies' ('ESICs'). The tax incentives are contained in Subdivision 360-A of the *Income Tax Assessment Act 1997* (Cth) ('ITAA 1997') and consist of a 'front-end' 20% tax offset, coupled with a 'back-end' 10 year capital gains tax ('CGT') exemption. To qualify for the incentives, a number of complex criteria must be satisfied by both the investor and the ESIC.

The ESI program operates alongside several pre-existing tax incentive programs that are aimed at encouraging formal venture capital investment in Australia. These programs were introduced over a number of years and are known as the Pooled Development Funds ('PDF') program, the Venture Capital Limited Partnership ('VCLP') program and the Early Stage Venture Capital Limited Partnership ('ESVCLP') program. The programs are highly regulated and provide a range of different kinds of tax incentives to eligible investors who invest in special kinds of

---

Portugal (Programa Semente), Slovenia (Corporate Income Tax Regime for companies under the Venture Capital Companies Act), South Korea (Tax Exemptions for Venture Capital Companies), Sweden (New Investment Incentive), Turkey (Business Angel Scheme), the United Kingdom (Venture Capital Trusts scheme) and the United States (Qualified Small Business Stock): at 98–103.

[15] *National Innovation and Science Agenda* (n 2).

[16] Some of the other measures announced in NISA included the establishment of the 'Biomedical Translation Fund' and the 'CSIRO Innovation Fund': ibid 7. These funds are designed to support the commercialisation of medical research and research emanating from CSIRO and other publicly funded research agencies. Both funds are co-investment funds, in which the Government invests alongside private sector investors. NISA also resulted in the introduction of an 'Incubator Support Programme': at 16. The Incubator Support Programme provides grant funding to incubators to deliver support services to Australian start-ups with an international focus. Grants are available to support new incubators in regions or sectors with high innovation potential, and for existing incubators that are planning to expand their services. The Incubator Support Programme forms an element of the 'Entrepreneurs' Programme', which provides various forms of support, including grants, to entrepreneurial businesses (see 4.2.2.1): Business.gov.au, *Entrepreneurs' Programme* (30 October 2018) <https://www.business.gov.au/assistance/entrepreneurs-programme>.

[17] StartupAUS, *Crossroads 2015 – An Action Plan to Develop a Vibrant Tech Startup Ecosystem in Australia* (Report, 2015) 2.

[18] *National Innovation and Science Agenda* (n 2) 1.

venture capital funds that have been registered by the relevant regulator (currently Innovation and Science Australia ('ISA')).[19]

The ESI program is a revolutionary new initiative, as this is the first time that the Australian Government has introduced tax incentives to encourage informal venture capital investment. Importantly, unlike the PDF, VCLP and ESVCLP programs, which provide tax incentives for indirect investment in start-ups through venture capital funds, the ESI program provides tax incentives for direct investment in such companies by angels and certain other eligible investors. In implementing this new initiative, Australia has followed the lead of several other countries around the world that have also implemented their own special kinds of angel tax incentives to stimulate investment in their start-up sectors.[20] Of particular interest is the United Kingdom's Seed Enterprise Investment Scheme' ('SEIS'), which was introduced in 2012 and was rated by the European Commission in 2017 as the best angel tax incentive in terms of good practice across 36 sample countries.[21] Australia's ESI program has been loosely modelled on the SEIS.[22] However, it also has a number of significant differences to its United Kingdom counterpart, making it quite a unique regime in its own right.

1.4 Aim and Structure of this Book

The aim of this book is to closely examine and critically analyse Australia's new ESI program in the context of the country's broader innovation system. The book discusses the policy rationale behind the introduction of the program and its position alongside Australia's pre-existing formal venture capital tax incentive programs. It also compares and contrasts the ESI program with the United Kingdom's SEIS and makes some suggestions for ways that the Australian program might possibly be reformed to better meet its policy objectives.

[19] ISA is an independent statutory body that works closely with the Department of Industry, Innovation and Science. It is responsible for regulating various aspects of Australia's formal venture capital tax incentive programs, as well as the R&D tax incentive (see 4.2.2.1). Interestingly, ISA does not have any direct role in regulating the ESI program. Instead, responsibility for the ESI program rests entirely with the Australian Taxation Office ('ATO'). It should be noted that the ATO is also responsible for administering certain aspects of Australia's formal venture capital programs as well as the R&D tax incentive.

[20] In this book, the term 'angel tax incentive' is used to describe an incentive that is available to individuals (although not necessarily exclusively to such persons) for investments made directly in start-ups rather than indirectly through venture capital funds. Some of the other countries around the world that have their own angel tax incentives include France, Germany, Israel, Italy, Japan, Portugal, Spain and Turkey: see European Commission (n 14) 135–40.

[21] These countries comprised the European Union nations as well as selected OECD countries: ibid 4, 202. The European Commission noted that the SEIS's ranking was driven by 'high scores across scope, qualifying criteria and administration': at 202. The rankings are discussed further at 5.10.

[22] National Innovation and Science Agenda (n 2) 6.

The remainder of the book is divided into the following chapters:

- **Chapter 2: Innovation, Start-Ups and Venture Capital.** Chapter 2 discusses the importance of innovation and the critical role that start-ups play in a country's innovation system. It also examines the nature of venture capital investment and outlines the key similarities and differences between angels and venture capitalists and the special roles they play in financing start-ups.
- **Chapter 3: Australia's Formal Venture Capital Tax Incentive Programs.** Chapter 3 examines the ways in which tax incentives have been used in Australia to support venture capital investment. It discusses some of the key considerations that governments should have in mind when designing venture capital tax incentive programs and examines some of the broad features of Australia's formal venture capital tax incentives.
- **Chapter 4: Australia's Early Stage Investor Program.** Chapter 4 focuses on the operation of the ESI program. It explains the policy rationale behind the introduction of the program and discusses its complex technical requirements in detail. Special attention is devoted to the program's 'early stage' and 'innovation' requirements, which are crucial for determining whether a start-up qualifies as an ESIC. The tax incentives available under the program are also discussed in detail and their benefits are closely scrutinised and evaluated.
- **Chapter 5: United Kingdom's Seed Enterprise Investment Scheme.** Chapter 5 examines the operation of the United Kingdom's SEIS. It compares the eligibility requirements of the SEIS with those of the ESI program and highlights some of the essential ways in which the programs differ. Particular attention is paid to the nature of the tax incentives available under the United Kingdom scheme, which are wider than those offered under the Australian program.
- **Chapter 6: Suggestions for Reforming Australia's Early Stage Investor Program.** Chapter 6 builds on the policy framework and comparative discussion set out in the previous chapters. It makes some suggestions for reforming the ESI program so that it might be able to better achieve its policy objectives. The suggestions draw on comparisons made between the ESI program and the SEIS, as well as various aspects of Australia's formal venture capital tax incentive programs.

As the programs discussed in this book are heavily regulated and based on complex technical legislative provisions, we have included a number of user-friendly diagrams, flowcharts and practical examples to help readers better understand how the programs operate. For ease of reference, we have also included an appendix at the end of the book containing the ESI provisions in Subdivision 360-A of the ITAA 1997.

The book is designed to serve as a practical guide to the ESI program, and deals with the law in force as at 1 December 2018.[23] It should be particularly useful to

[23] It also considers a set of proposed legislative amendments to the ESI program contained in Treasury Laws Amendment (2018 Measures No. 2) Bill 2018 (Cth). This Bill was introduced into the Commonwealth Parliament in February 2018 and was before the Senate at the time of writing.

entrepreneurs who are seeking finance for their start-ups, angels who wish to access the generous tax incentives provided under the program, and legal and financial advisers who assist these parties. Academics and students involved in the areas of entrepreneurship, innovation and venture capital should also find the book a valuable resource for their broader scholarly research. Finally, the book should be of specific interest to government policymakers and regulators who are involved in designing and administering innovation and venture capital programs.

References

Australian Government, *Industry Innovation and Competitiveness Agenda – An Action Plan for a Stronger Australia* (Report, 2014)

Australian Government, *National Innovation and Science Agenda – Welcome to the Ideas Boom* (Report, November 2015)

Australian Government, Department of Industry, Innovation and Science, Office of the Chief Economist, *Australian Innovation System Report 2017* (Report, 2017)

Barkoczy, Stephen and Daniel Sandler, *Government Venture Capital Incentives: A Multi-Jurisdiction Comparative Analysis* (Australian Tax Research Foundation, 2007)

Barkoczy, Stephen, Tamara Wilkinson, Ann Monotti and Mark Davison, *Innovation and Venture Capital Law and Policy* (Federation Press, 2016)

Brechbühl, Beat A and Bob Wooder, 'General Report' in Beat A Brechbühl and Bob Wooder (eds), *Global Venture Capital Transactions: A Practical Approach* (Kluwer Law International, 2004)

Business.gov.au, *Entrepreneurs' Programme* (30 October 2018) <https://www.business.gov.au/assistance/entrepreneurs-programme>

Decker, Ryan, John Haltiwanger, Ron Jarmin, and Javier Miranda, 'The Role of Entrepreneurship in US Job Creation and Economic Dynamism' (2014) 28(3) *Journal of Economic Perspectives* 3

Diaz-Moriana, Vanessa, and Colm O'Gorman, 'Informal Investors and the Informal Venture Capital Market in Ireland' (2013) 3(6) *Journal of Asian Scientific Research* 630

Directorate-General for Research and Innovation, *State of the Innovation Union 2015* (European Commission Report, 2015)

Edler, Jakob and Jan Fagerberg, 'Innovation Policy: What, Why and How' (2017) 33(1) *Oxford Review of Economic Policy* 2

European Commission, 'Effectiveness of Tax Incentives for Venture Capital and Business Angels to Foster the Investment of SMEs and Start-ups: Final Report' (Working Paper No 68, European Commission, June 2017)

Lerner, Josh, *Boulevard of Broken Dreams: Why Public Efforts to Boost Entrepreneurship and Venture Capital Have Failed – and What to Do About It* (Princeton University Press, 2009)

OECD, *Financing High-Growth Firms – The Role of Angel Investors* (OECD, 2011)

OECD, *Innovation and Growth: Rationale for an Innovation Strategy* (Report, 2007)

Scheela, William, Edmundo Isidro, Thawatchai Jittrapanun and Nguyen Thi Thu Trang, 'Formal and Informal Venture Capital Investing in Emerging Economies in Southeast Asia' (2015) 32(3) *Asia Pacific Journal of Management* 597

Spender, John-Christopher, Vincenzo Corvello, Michele Grimaldi and Pierluigi Rippa, 'Startups and Open Innovation: A Review of the Literature' (2017) 20(1) *European Journal of Innovation Management* 4

StartupAUS, *Crossroads 2015 – An Action Plan to Develop a Vibrant Tech Startup Ecosystem in Australia* (Report, 2015)

StartupAUS, *Crossroads – An Action Plan to Develop a Vibrant Tech Startup Ecosystem in Australia* (Report, 2016)
StartupAUS, *Crossroads: An Action Plan to Develop a World-Leading Tech Startup Ecosystem in Australia* (Report, 2017)
Treasury and Department of Industry, Innovation, Science, Research and Tertiary Education, *Review of Venture Capital and Entrepreneurial Skills* (Final Report, 2012)
Treasury Laws Amendment (2018 Measures No. 2) Bill 2018 (Cth)

Chapter 2
Innovation, Start-Ups and Venture Capital

Abstract Innovation involves the creation of new and improved products, processes and services. It is about doing things in new and clever ways that increase efficiency and add value. Although Australia is a clever country that has world-class universities, respected research agencies and pioneering scientific institutes, its entrepreneurs have often struggled to commercialise their innovations. This has been attributed to a number of factors, including a lack of venture capital funding being available to start-ups. Venture capital is a scarce resource because it is an extremely risky investment that can take many years to provide returns for investors. The venture capital market is highly sensitive to economic conditions and is often disproportionately affected during downturns. Angels and venture capitalists are the two main sources of venture capital funding for start-ups. While it is the founders of start-ups that come up with the revolutionary ideas for new products and services, it is angels and venture capitalists who provide the finance necessary to develop and commercialise these ideas. Angels and venture capitalists are therefore key actors in a country's innovation system, even though they are not necessarily innovators themselves. By providing much needed capital to start-ups, these investors share in the risks associated with these companies. This chapter discusses the importance of innovation and the critical role that start-ups play in a country's innovation system. It also examines the nature of venture capital investment and the special roles that angels and venture capitalists play in financing start-ups.

2.1 Introduction

Innovation has become one of the most popular, and arguably overused, business buzzwords in the English language.[1] The finance literature is peppered with a myriad of different definitions of this term. The OECD, for example, describes

[1] James Hyndman, *Let's Stop Using the Word 'Innovation'* (9 April 2018) Quinn Allan <https://www.quinnallan.com.au/market-news-item/lets-stop-using-word-innovation/>; Edmund Tadros, 'Innovation a Mere Buzzword for More Than Half of Firms', *Australian Financial Review* (online),

S. Barkoczy, T. Wilkinson, *Incentivising Angels*, SpringerBriefs in Law,
https://doi.org/10.1007/978-981-13-6632-1_2

innovation as 'the implementation of a new or significantly improved product (good or service), or process, a new marketing method, or a new organisational method in business practices, workplace organisation or external relations'.[2] By way of contrast, Microsoft Corporation has defined innovation as 'the conversion of knowledge and ideas into new or improved products, processes, or services to gain a competitive advantage'.[3] Irrespective of whichever definition one uses, it is widely accepted that innovation is a catalyst that stimulates business growth and provides many benefits to a nation, including productivity gains and improved living standards.[4]

Innovation is important for all sectors of the economy, and helps a nation remain competitive and at the cutting edge.[5] It also 'delivers substantial benefits to society's well-being and is key to solving some of its most pressing challenges'.[6] The process of innovation is continuous[7] and multi-faceted,[8] and can cover a wide range of activities.[9] Innovation begins with the novel ideas of individuals, and can involve 'an

---

27 June 2017 <https://www.afr.com/business/accounting/innovation-a-mere-buzzword-for-more-than-half-of-firms-20170625-gwyabb>.

[2] OECD, *OSLO Manual: Guidelines for Collecting and Interpreting Innovation Data* (OECD, 3rd ed, 2005) 46. This definition has been adopted in various Australian Government reports, see e.g., Australian Government, Department of Industry, Innovation and Science, Office of the Chief Economist, *Australian Innovation System Report 2017* (Report, 2017) 7, 114 ('*Australian Innovation System Report 2017*'). It has also been relied on in designing the 'principles-based test' in the ESI program (see 4.2.2.2).

[3] Microsoft, 'Best Practices for Innovation: Microsoft's Innovation Management Framework' (Microsoft Corporation, June 2013) 5.

[4] Chandrajit Banerjee, 'The Human Factor: The Fundamental Driver of Innovation' in Soumitra Dutta, Bruno Lanvin and Sacha Wunsch-Vincent (eds), *Global Innovation Index 2014 – The Human Factor in Innovation* (Cornell University, INSEAD and WIPO, 2014) vii; HM Treasury and the Department for Business Innovation & Skills, 'Our Plan for Growth: Science and Innovation' (December 2014) 53; Richard R Nelson, *The Sources of Economic Growth* (Harvard University Press, 2000); Daniele Archibugi, Jeremy Howells and Jonathan Michie (eds), *Innovation Policy in a Global Economy* (Cambridge University Press, 2003); Christine Greenhalgh and Mark Rogers, *Innovation, Intellectual Property, and Economic Growth* (Princeton University Press, 2010); Bronwyn H Hall and Nathan Rosenberg (eds), *Handbook of the Economics of Innovation: Volumes 1 and 2* (Elsevier, 2010).

[5] Australian Government, *National Innovation and Science Agenda – Welcome to the Ideas Boom* (Report, November 2015) 1 ('*National Innovation and Science Agenda*').

[6] *Australian Innovation System Report 2017* (n 2) 6.

[7] OECD, *OSLO Manual: Guidelines for Collecting and Interpreting Innovation Data* (n 2) 15.

[8] See Jean-Philippe Deschamps, 'Innovation and Leadership' in Larisa V Shavinina (ed), *The International Handbook on Innovation* (Elsevier Science, 2003) 824; Jan Fagerberg, David C Mowery and Richard R Nelson, *The Oxford Handbook of Innovation* (Oxford University Press, 2005) v; David L Rainey, *Product Innovation: Leading Change through Integrated Product Development* (Cambridge University Press, 2005) x.

[9] For instance, the innovation process can include activities from 'identifying problems and generating new ideas and solutions, to implementing new solutions and diffusing new technologies': Itzhak Goldberg, John Gabriel Goddard, Smita Kuriakose and Jean-Louis Racine, *Igniting Innovation – Rethinking the Role of Government in Emerging Europe and Central Asia* (Report, World Bank, 2011) 20.

enormous amount of uncertainty, human creativity, and chance'.[10] Ultimately, innovation is all about 'thinking outside the box' – it involves developing practical solutions to address deficiencies in products and services, and applying new knowledge to do things 'in clever ways that are often cheaper, faster and more effective than the ways in which they were previously done'.[11]

It has often been said that research and development ('R&D') plays an important role in a country's innovation system.[12] While much R&D often goes into creating innovations, R&D by itself does not constitute innovation; it is simply an 'input' into innovation.[13] For R&D to become an innovation it needs to be applied in creating or improving products and processes. On this basis, although R&D is often used as an indicator or proxy of innovation, businesses need to undertake the additional step of implementing and commercialising their R&D activities in order to actually turn them into innovations.

According to the World Bank, innovation should be construed broadly as 'something that is new relative to a given context'.[14] An innovation may therefore be 'new to the country in which it appears, to the region or the sector in which it takes place, or to the firm that develops or adopts it'.[15] Innovations come in all shapes and sizes and should not be limited purely to scientific and technological innovations.[16] Although most innovations usually involve only small incremental improvements, some innovations are so ground-breaking that they spawn revolutionary new industries that end up changing society forever.[17]

---

[10] James M Utterback, *Mastering the Dynamics of Innovation* (Harvard Business School Press, 1994) vii.

[11] Stephen Barkoczy, Tamara Wilkinson, Ann Monotti and Mark Davison, *Innovation and Venture Capital Law and Policy* (Federation Press, 2016) 20. It is worth noting that although most innovations result in only small incremental changes, others can completely revolutionise industries.

[12] *Australian Innovation System Report 2017* (n 2) 71. However, it needs to be acknowledged that the importance of R&D varies by industry.

[13] Ibid.

[14] World Bank, *Innovation Policy – A Guide for Developing Countries* (World Bank, 2010) 54.

[15] Ibid.

[16] It has been noted that: 'Novel ideas can come from anywhere and they can be applied to any field of human endeavour': *Australian Innovation System Report 2017* (n 2) 6.

[17] Ground-breaking new devices such as Apple's iPad and iPhone have completely revolutionised the computing and telecommunications industries and have given birth to new industries such as the software 'apps' industry: see further, Pai-Ling Yin, Jason P Davis and Yulia Muzyrya, 'Entrepreneurial Innovation: Killer Apps in the iPhone Ecosystem' (2014) 104 (5) *American Economic Review* 255. Over the last decade, the apps industry has witnessed explosive growth. There are now millions of different apps available to both iOS and android users and hundreds of millions of downloads taking place each year: Artyom Dogtiev, *App Download and Usage Statistics* (8 October 2018) Business of Apps <http://www.businessofapps.com/data/app-statistics/>; Sam Costello, *How Many Apps Are in the App Store?* (7 April 2018) Lifewire <https://www.lifewire.com/how-many-apps-in-app-store-2000252>.

2.2 Australia and the Global Innovation Race

The Australian Government has recognised that it is crucial for Australia's economic prosperity that it is an innovative nation with 'a culture that backs good ideas and learns from taking risks and making mistakes'.[18] This, in turn, requires a strong research and entrepreneurial environment that is supported by the availability of adequate sources of funding necessary to 'turn ideas into innovative outputs'.[19] Although Australia is a clever country that has world-class universities,[20] respected research agencies[21] and pioneering scientific institutes,[22] the reality is that its entrepreneurs have often struggled to successfully commercialise their innovations.[23] The reasons for Australia's patchy commercialisation track-record are not entirely clear, but one factor that has been consistently identified as a problem is the lack of adequate sources of venture capital finance being available to start-ups.[24] Without venture capital, many start-ups are forced to abandon their projects or go overseas to places like Silicon Valley in order to seek funding. This puts Australia at risk of losing its aspiring entrepreneurs and missing out on the many spillover benefits that start-ups can bring to the national economy.

Developing effective programs that support the special needs of the start-up sector is therefore an important matter for the Australian Government to consider in the

---

[18] *National Innovation and Science Agenda* (n 5) 1.

[19] Treasury and Department of Industry, Innovation, Science, Research and Tertiary Education, *Review of Venture Capital and Entrepreneurial Skills* (Final Report, 2012) 13.

[20] Australia has 'an enviable reputation as a destination of choice for international students seeking a high quality university education', with international education being the country's third largest export: Universities Australia, 'Keep it Clever' (Policy Statement 2016, 7 October 2015) 3. In a recent report, Australia's higher education system was ranked 10th out of 50 nations: Ross Williams, Anne Leahy, Gaétan de Rassenfosse and Paul Jensen, *U21 Ranking of National Higher Education Systems 2015* (Report, Melbourne Institute of Applied Economic and Social Research, May 2015) 8. The Australian university sector is led by the 'Go8' universities, which are a group of eight research intensive universities. Six of these universities (the University of Melbourne, Australian National University, the University of Sydney, the University of Queensland, Monash University and the University of New South Wales) were ranked in the top 100 universities in the world in 2018: Times Higher Education, *World University Rankings 2018* (2018) <https://www.timeshighereducation.com/world-university-rankings/2018/world-ranking#!/page/0/length/100/sort_by/scores_overall/sort_order/asc/cols/scores>.

[21] Australia's leading research agencies include Commonwealth Scientific and Industrial Research Organisation (CSIRO), the Australian Research Council and the National Health and Medical Research Council.

[22] These institutes include the Florey Institute of Neuroscience and Mental Health, the Garvan Institute of Medical Research, the Peter MacCallum Cancer Centre, the Victor Chang Cardiac Research Institute and the Walter and Eliza Hall Institute of Medical Research.

[23] *National Innovation and Science Agenda* (n 5) 4; W D Ferris, 'Australia Chooses: Venture Capital and a Future Australia' (2001) 26 (Special Issue) *Australian Journal of Management* 45, 47, 51.

[24] Ferris (n 23) 47, 49. According to the Australia Government, around '4500 startups miss out on equity finance each year': *National Innovation and Science Agenda* (n 5) 6.

design of its broader innovation policies.[25] Unless Australia backs its entrepreneurs, it stands to fall behind many other countries that are all actively competing in a high-stakes 'global innovation race'.[26] In order to have the brightest possible economic future, Australia needs to be at the forefront of this race so that it can reap the many tantalising opportunities that innovation can bring. These opportunities include a larger share of global wealth, better jobs and greater access to innovative products and services.[27]

Unfortunately, Australia has been lagging behind many other OECD countries in various innovation indicators, such as gross expenditure on research and development ('GERD').[28] In this regard, it is interesting to note that while Australian businesses spent $18.9 billion on R&D in 2013–14, they only spent $16.7 billion on R&D in 2015–16.[29] In terms of its overall innovation ranking, Australia was ranked 20th out of 126 countries in the *Global Innovation Index 2018*.[30] When this ranking is broken down further, it is noteworthy that Australia performed poorly in some of the key sub-indicators, such as 38th for its knowledge and technology outputs and 69th for its graduates in science and engineering.[31] If Australia wants to succeed in being a leading innovative nation in the twenty-first century, it needs to improve its performance. As Bill Ferris, the former Chair of Innovation and Science Australia, has warned:

> Looking towards 2030, innovation will be integral to the expansion of Australia's economy, keeping its workforce strong, and addressing societal challenges. Australia will need to be competitive in a global innovation race by scaling up more high-growth industries and companies; commercialising more high-value products and services; fostering great talent; and daring to tackle global challenges.
>
> Yet just at the time when Australia needs to accelerate its innovation performance, we are falling behind our global peers, particularly in student performance in science and mathematics, and in business investment in research and development. This is more than a canary chirp in our economic mineshaft: it is a clarion call for national action.[32]

---

[25] The Productivity Commission has recognised that '[t]he rationale for government support of start-ups is that they create knowledge and network spillovers that benefit other businesses and the wider community, resulting in a "virtuous" cycle of entrepreneurship, innovation, investment, income and employment growth': Productivity Commission, *Business Set-up, Transfer and Closure* (Report No 75, Productivity Commission, 30 September 2015) 253.

[26] Innovation and Science Australia, *Australia 2030: Prosperity Through Innovation* (Report, November 2017) 1.

[27] Ibid.

[28] OECD, *Main Science and Technology Indicators* (2017) <https://stats.oecd.org/Index.aspx?DataSetCode=MSTI_PUB>. GERD 'represents the total expenditure devoted to R&D by the business, government, private non-profit and higher education sectors': *Australian Innovation System Report 2017* (n 2) 114.

[29] *Australian Innovation System Report 2017* (n 2) 70.

[30] Soumitra Dutta, Bruno Lanvin and Sacha Wunsch-Vincent (eds), *Global Innovation Index 2018 – Energizing the World with Innovation* (11th edition, Cornell University, INSEAD and WIPO, 2018) xx.

[31] Ibid 222.

[32] Innovation and Science Australia (n 26) iii.

2.3 Start-Up Companies as Drivers of Innovation

Although innovation can take place within all sorts of companies and at many different points in their life cycles, it is traditionally start-ups that tend to have the most innovative businesses and the greatest prospects for growth. For the purposes of this book, a start-up may be broadly defined as a company that is at an early stage of development, has high growth potential, and is involved in developing and commercialising some new form of product or service.[33] Start-ups are dynamic companies, and the entrepreneurs that found them often possess special scientific, technological or creative skills and have the ability to see business opportunities that others might have missed. These companies are often involved in niche markets and are typically heavily engaged in R&D activities as well as prototyping and testing their products and services. Start-ups often have not yet recruited all their key staff and generally have relatively few tangible assets against which they can borrow money. In many cases, their major asset is some form of intellectual property that they have developed, such as a patent. The value of such property is, however, generally hard to ascertain as its commercial applications and market potential may not yet be known.

Start-ups are exciting companies because they often have disruptive and transformational technologies. Their entrepreneurial nature means that they have the potential to generate new kinds of employment, revolutionise industries and create derivative businesses.[34] Their capacity to innovate and grow rapidly allows them to deliver greater 'bang for the buck' than other companies. This makes them an important sector of a country's knowledge-based economy. Successful start-ups help foster entrepreneurship by laying the seeds for the creation of other start-ups that seek to emulate them.

Importantly, while start-ups come with high levels of risk, they also have the potential to generate high levels of return for their founders and those who are bold enough to invest in them at such an early stage of their development. The reality is that many of the largest and most successful companies in the world commenced their lives as humble start-ups. There are countless well-known examples of these companies, including global icons such as the technology giants Apple, Google and Facebook. While not all start-ups achieve success, those that do often end up making significant contributions to both society and the economy.

---

[33] It has been observed that start-ups 'start small but have the capacity to experience massive and sustained growth, often enabling them to become significant players in global industries within a small number of years': StartupAUS, *Crossroads 2015 – An Action Plan to Develop a Vibrant Tech Startup Ecosystem in Australia* (Report, 2015) 10.

[34] Sohin Shah, 'How Disruptive Startups Spread the Wealth by Encouraging Derivative Businesses', *Entrepreneur* (online), 3 June 2015 <http://www.entrepreneur.com/article/246783>.

2.3.1 *Contrasting Start-Ups with Other Small Businesses*

Although start-ups fall within the general small business umbrella, it is important to recognise that only a tiny proportion of small businesses are actually start-ups.[35] Start-ups lie at one end of the small business spectrum. They comprise those early stage companies that 'are highly innovative, have ambitious growth expectations and a desire "to change the way things are done"'.[36] At the other end of the small business spectrum are those companies that tend to 'satisfy a lifestyle choice and/or primarily seek to provide stable employment and income for the owners and their families'.[37] These companies constitute the bulk of small businesses and, unlike start-ups, do not generally play a significant role in a country's innovation system. While it is unquestionable that they also make valuable contributions to a nation's economy, they differ from start-ups in that they are primarily consumers of innovation rather than creators of innovation.

2.3.2 *Contrasting Start-Ups with Large Businesses*

Start-ups are not the only kinds of companies that are innovative. Many large companies are also actively engaged in innovation. However, these companies are in a very different position to start-ups as they usually have the requisite experience and superior resources necessary to undertake their R&D and commercialisation activities. Large companies already have established businesses with products and services in the market to provide them with regular income streams. They are also more likely to have significant tangible assets against which they can secure funding for their projects. In contrast to large companies, start-ups face a number of special challenges. In particular, as they do not usually have positive cash flows, start-ups usually require significant injections of capital to pursue their business plans. They also generally need to get their products and services to market within a very short time frame in order to avoid being overtaken by larger companies and losing their competitive advantage. Timing is therefore crucial for start-ups, and anything that holds up their development, especially a lack of finance, can be fatal to their future prospects. In this regard, it has been noted that:

> It is start-up and early stage companies that usually face the greatest headwinds and are at the greatest risk of failure. Not surprisingly, because of their risky nature and limited

[35] The Productivity Commission has estimated that less than 0.5% of Australia's new businesses are start-ups: Productivity Commission (n 25) 4.

[36] Ibid 3.

[37] Ibid. In contrast to start-ups which have emerging high-growth businesses, traditional small businesses tend to have 'less differentiated products or services', are 'often trading in a confined geographical area', and will remain small even if they experience growth: StartupAUS, *Crossroads – An Action Plan to Develop a Vibrant Tech Startup Ecosystem in Australia* (Report, 2016) 22.

resources, these companies are also precisely the ones that typically require venture capital investment and stand to benefit the most from government support.[38]

2.4 The Nature of Venture Capital

The Australian Government defines venture capital as 'high-risk private equity capital for typically new, innovative or fast growing unlisted companies'.[39] Venture capital investment traditionally takes place at what are commonly known as the 'pre-seed', 'seed', 'start-up' and 'early-expansion' stages of a company's life cycle.[40] The early stages at which such investment is made means that it is an innately risky form of finance as there is a high possibility that the investee company will not be successful. As venture capital investors hold equity in a company, they rank behind lenders in winding up proceedings and stand to lose their whole investment if the company fails. In addition, as start-ups are typically unlisted, it can be extremely difficult for investors to exit their investments. The illiquid nature of private company shares means that venture capital investors often have to spend considerable time locating and negotiating with potential buyers before they can exit their investments. They also need to ensure that their investee companies have grown enough so that they have reached the stage of development where they are attractive to the next round of investors.

For the reasons outlined above, it is not surprising that venture capital is a scarce commodity that is extremely sensitive to economic conditions. In practice, it is not unusual for venture capital funding to quickly 'dry up' in unstable environments, where investors traditionally gravitate towards less risky asset classes.[41] Venture

---

[38] Barkoczy et al. (n 11) 5.

[39] *Australian Innovation System Report 2017* (n 2) 118.

[40] See Treasury and Department of Industry, Innovation, Science, Research and Tertiary Education (n 19) 13. While the precise definitions of the various stages vary widely, the Australian Bureau of Statistics has set out some features that identify them. It notes that a company in the pre-seed stage is generally in the process of setting up, and its products are at the testing or pilot production stage. A company will generally be in the seed stage if it is in the process of setting up and its products are in the R&D stage. A company in the start-up stage will generally not yet be fully operational, even though it may or may not be generating revenue. Finally, a company will be in the early expansion stage if it is operational and has a product in the market place. It will generally show significant revenue growth, and may or may not be profitable: Australian Bureau of Statistics, '5678.0 – Venture Capital and Later Stage Private Equity, Australia, 2016–17' (28 February 2018) <http://www.abs.gov.au/AUSSTATS/abs@.nsf/Latestproducts/5678.0Main%20Features12016-17?opendocument&tabname=Summary&prodno=5678.0&issue=2016-17&num=&view=>.

[41] The OECD has noted that venture capital, along with expenditure on R&D, is 'among the first expenditures to be cut during recessions in OECD countries': OECD, *Science, Technology and Industry Scoreboard 2009* (OECD, 2009) 7.

capital activity therefore tends to move in 'boom and bust' cycles.[42] Periods of decreased venture capital investment are often triggered by 'black swan' events, such as the 2000 'tech wreck' and the 2008 'global financial crisis'.[43] It can take many years for a country's venture capital sector to recover after such incidents, and it often takes generous government incentives to lure investors back into the market.

2.5 Angels and Venture Capitalists

As mentioned in Chap. 1, angels and venture capitalists are the two main sources of venture capital funding for start-ups.[44] While angels and venture capitalists share a number of common features, they are quite distinct kinds of investors. The key similarities and differences between these two kinds of investors are discussed below and examined further in subsequent chapters.

---

[42] Christopher C Golis, Patrick D Mooney and Thomas F Richardson, *Enterprise and Venture Capital: A Business Builders' and Investors' Handbook* (Allen and Unwin, 5th ed, 2009) xxi; Douglas Cumming, 'Introduction' in Douglas Cumming (ed), *The Oxford Handbook of Venture Capital* (Oxford University Press, 2012) 2.

[43] The adverse impact that the global financial crisis had on access to finance for Australian businesses has been widely recognised in various reports: see e.g., Productivity Commission (n 25) 124. In particular, it has been noted that the global financial crisis led to a slowdown in lending to small businesses and a widening of interest rate margins in Australia: Senate Economics References Committee, *Access of Small Business to Finance* (Report, 30 June 2010) 1.

[44] It is worth noting that there are also two other less-commonly discussed sources of venture capital funding for start-ups, namely 'corporate venture capital' and 'university venture capital': see generally Barkoczy et al. (n 11) 45–8. Corporate venture capital involves large companies investing in start-ups through their in-house venture capital funds. Engaging in corporate venture capital allows companies to stay abreast of new developments and facilitate the early acquisition of new technologies from potential future competitors. Some of the world's most active corporate venture capital investors include Intel Capital, Google Ventures, Cisco Investments, GE Ventures and Microsoft Ventures: Australian Private Equity and Venture Capital Association Limited, *The Venture Capital Effect: A Report on the Industry's Impact on the Australian Economy* (Report, 13 June 2017) 59. University venture capital, on the other hand, involves universities funding start-ups that have been created by their researchers and spun out of their institutions. While investment of this type may provide financial returns for the university, it also allows research developed within the university to be disseminated, which can provide significant reputational benefits. Universities such as Stanford, Harvard and MIT are famous for their spin out technology companies that contributed to the establishment of famous venture capital hubs in the United States such as Silicon Valley and Route 128. In the Australian context, it is interesting to note that Monash University and the University of Melbourne, with the support of the Victorian Government, have recently established BioCurate, a new $80 million fund to support early-stage biomedical research: see *BioCurate* <http://www.biocurate.com>.

2.5.1 Similarities Between Angels and Venture Capitalists

What is common about angels and venture capitalists is that they are both sophisticated investors who focus on investing in emerging, entrepreneurial companies at the early stages of their life cycle. Angels and venture capitalists are frequently approached by start-ups seeking finance, and also actively use their own networks to seek out promising companies. They generally perform due diligence on those companies in which they wish to make investments and tend to only select a small portfolio of companies that meet their metrics. Angels and venture capitalists closely monitor their investees and often provide funding in stages based on how the companies are progressing with their business plans and whether or not they are meeting key milestones. They are savvy investors who protect their investments by imposing strict conditions on their investees and insist on being granted special rights under their shareholders' agreements.[45]

Angels and venture capitalists tend to also be active investors who help build their investee companies' businesses. In order to maximise their potential returns, they often spend significant amounts of time working with their investees, advising them and guiding their development. This active and engaged mentoring is a unique aspect of venture capital finance that differentiates it from other forms of investment. The level and quality of mentoring support obtained by a start-up is often a critical element in its ultimate success.

As start-ups are rarely cash-flow positive, they tend to reinvest any revenue they make back into their businesses, so it is unusual for them to pay dividends to their shareholders. This means that, in practice, the principal way that venture capital investors generally make returns from their investments is by exiting them. Exits tend to take place only once a start-up has achieved a critical stage of growth. They can occur in a number of ways, including through 'trade sales',[46] 'management

[45] These rights are designed to give investors greater control over their investee companies. They often include 'board rights' (which enable the investor to sit on the company's board), 'veto rights' (which limit major strategic, operational or financial decisions being made without the investor's consent) 'drag-along rights' (which enable the investor to compel the other investors in a company to sell their shares along with the investor's shares to a third party purchaser), 'demand rights' (which allow the investor to force a company to become listed on a stock exchange), and 'pre-emptive rights' (which give the investor a first right of refusal to buy new shares issued by the company): see Barkoczy et al. (n 11) 57–8.

[46] Trade sales are one of the most common ways that venture capital investors exit their investments. They involve a 'trade buyer' (who may be a third party or an existing investor in the company) purchasing the venture capital investor's shares in the company. While trade sales have historically been seen as a less lucrative exit method than an initial public offering, they often prove to be extremely successful. See further: ibid 67; Bruce Booth, 'Acquisitions as the Silent Partner in Biotech Liquidity: IPO vs. M&A Exit Paths', *Forbes* (online), 27 October 2014 <https://www.forbes.com/sites/brucebooth/2014/10/27/acquisitions-as-the-silent-partner-in-biotech-liquidity-ipo-vs-ma-exit-paths/#727853073561>; A Gruener and R Kutz, 'Trade Sale versus IPO as Exit Strategy – An Empirical Analysis of European and US VC Backed Biotechnology Companies' (2017) 1 (4) *Austin Journal of Business Administration and Management* 1; Agnes King and Caitlin Fitzsimmons, 'How the Mathematics of Venture Capital Has Changed and What

buy-outs' ('MBOs')[47] and 'initial public offerings' ('IPOs').[48] Getting a company to the stage where an investor can successfully exit their investment can, however, take many years, and for this reason venture capital is often referred to as 'patient capital'.

Although the risky nature of investing in start-ups means that angels and venture capitalists tend to have a high number of failed investments,[49] the spectacular returns that they can generate from their few successes can significantly outweigh their many losses.[50] In this regard, venture capital involves a 'high-risk/high-gain scenario' in which 'investors stand to either make phenomenal returns or suffer monumental failures'.[51]

2.5.2 Differences Between Angels and Venture Capitalists

Although angels and venture capitalists share the common goal of investing early in a company's life and making spectacular returns on exiting their investments, it is important to recognise that they are quite distinct kinds of investors with their own particular characteristics. The key difference between angels and venture capitalists

it Means for Start-Up Exits', *Australian Financial Review* (online), 18 March 2015 <https://www.afr.com/it-pro/how-the-mathematics-of-venture-capital-has-changed-and-what-it-means-for-startup-exits-20150318-1m22dq>.

[47] An MBO involves the existing management team of the company buying out the investors' shares to take complete control of the company: see further Barkoczy et al. (n 11) 68.

[48] An IPO involves listing a company on a stock exchange. IPOs have traditionally been seen as the best outcome for exiting a venture capital investment. Listing on a stock exchange is a lengthy and expensive process that can be achieved by only the most successful start-ups. Once the company has listed, its shares are publicly traded and are therefore more liquid. This makes it easier for investors to subsequently sell the shares: see further ibid 68–9.

[49] Angels and venture capitalists also tend to hold a number of 'zombie' investments. These are investments in companies that remain in existence after venture capital funding has run out, but which have stagnated and show no signs of growth. Zombie investments are unattractive for angels and venture capitalists to retain as they have not achieved their growth targets and can be difficult to exit: see further, Calvin H Johnson, 'Why Do Venture Capital Funds Burn Research and Development Deductions' (2009) 29 (1) *Virginia Tax Review* 29, 41–42; Jim Duffy, 'Zombie Start-ups: Why are Entrepreneurs Failing to Grow their Businesses?' *The Guardian* (online), 7 August 2017 <https://www.theguardian.com/small-business-network/2017/aug/07/zombie-start-ups-entrepreneurs-failing-grow-businesses>; Sathvik Tantry, *How Venture Capital Incentives Promote Zombie Companies* (7 August 2015) TechCrunch <https://techcrunch.com/2015/08/06/how-venture-capital-incentives-promote-zombie-companies/>; Sam Hogg, 'Zombie VC Firms Can Be an Entrepreneur's Nightmare', *Entrepreneur* (online), 31 October 2013 <https://www.entrepreneur.com/article/227925>.

[50] It has been noted that venture capital investors 'accept greater risk' than other investors, and consequently also 'hope for a higher return': John H Spillman, 'United States of America' in Beat A Brechbühl and Bob Wooder (eds), *Global Venture Capital Transactions: A Practical Approach* (Kluwer Law International, 2004) 313–4.

[51] Barkoczy et al. (n 11) 40.

is that angels act on their own behalf and invest their own money, whereas venture capitalists are professional fund managers who act on behalf of their investors whose money they invest.

Angels are typically wealthy business people who have often been former entrepreneurs themselves. As many angels are keen to 'give back' to the business community and pass on their knowledge to aspiring entrepreneurs, there can be a personal, and sometimes even altruistic, dimension to the kinds of investments they make.[52] Because angels tend to have less capital at their disposal than venture capitalists, they generally invest smaller amounts in fewer companies. They also tend to invest at an earlier stage of a start-up's development. In many cases, angel investment is a start-up's first injection of third party capital.[53]

Although angels generally invest by themselves, it is not uncommon for groups of angels to invest together in 'syndicates'.[54] Syndicates allow angels to spread their risk by investing in a larger portfolio of companies. They also allow angels to share the work of undertaking due diligence and monitoring investees, which can be quite time consuming and onerous. In addition, by investing in a syndicate, angels have the capacity to pool their capital and compete more equally in funding rounds with venture capitalists who tend to have more capital at their disposal.

Angel investment has been described as one of the 'most common, but least studied' methods of financing start-up companies.[55] This is not surprising as angel investors can be quite secretive about their investments. This means that data on angel investment levels in Australia is particularly scant.[56] The angel market is nevertheless a vital part of the innovation system, particularly as it supports companies at the earliest stages of development where the availability of capital is usually at its scarcest.

In contrast to angels, venture capitalists are intermediaries who operate venture capital funds on behalf of a group of investors from whom they raise and pool capital.[57] The investors in their funds usually include wealthy individuals and family

---

[52] See OECD, *Financing High-Growth Firms – The Role of Angel Investors* (OECD, 2011) 33 ('*Financing High Growth Firms*'); Joseph W Bartlett, *Fundamentals of Venture Capital* (Madison Books, 1999) 12; Dylan Democrat Damon, 'The Legal Aspects of Venture Capital Agreements: Part I' (2007) 25 *Companies and Securities Law Journal* 43, 44.

[53] Third party capital relates to external capital (i.e., capital that does not come from the entrepreneur or their family and friends).

[54] *Financing High Growth Firms* (n 52) 32–6.

[55] Andrew Wong, Mihir Bhatia and Zachary Freeman, 'Angel Finance: The Other Venture Capital' (2009) 18 *Strategic Change* 221, 229.

[56] StartupAUS, *Crossroads: An Action Plan to Develop a World-Leading Tech Startup Ecosystem in Australia* (Report, 2017) 67; Dominic Powell, 'Sydney Angels Reveals Investment Data: 54 Startups Have Received $193 Million Since 2008', *Smart Company*, 18 December 2017 <https://www.smartcompany.com.au/startupsmart/news-analysis/sydney-angels-reveals-investment-data/>.

[57] While venture capitalists primarily invest other peoples' money, they sometimes also invest their own money in the funds they manage. This signals to investors that they have 'skin in the game', which can sometimes help them raise capital.

offices as well as institutional investors like banks and superannuation funds. Venture capitalists generally work in skilled and experienced teams[58] and usually invest in a broader portfolio of companies than angels. The number of investments venture capitalists make typically depends on the size of their funds. While investing in more companies diversifies their portfolios and thereby decreases risk, it also increases the amount of work that venture capitalists have to do to monitor and support their investees. In practice, venture capitalists tend to invest at a slightly later stage than angels and their investments will often supplement existing angel investment in a company.[59] Because venture capitalists tend to have more resources than angels, they also tend to make larger investments and participate in more follow-on investment rounds than angels.[60]

Being professional fund managers, venture capitalists generally charge their investors periodic management fees for managing their funds.[61] In addition, they are also usually entitled to performance bonuses if they produce strong returns. These performance bonuses are known as 'carried interest payments' and are usually calculated as a specified percentage of the profits made from the fund's investments.[62] Carried interest payments give fund managers a 'stake' in a fund's profits, thereby aligning their interests with those of the investors who have contributed the capital. This reward operates as a strong incentive for fund managers to make good investment decisions.

[58] A venture capital team generally includes an eclectic mix of individuals with a diverse range of skills. For instance, teams often include entrepreneurs, lawyers, accountants, bankers and scientists.

[59] It has been suggested that one of the most important ways that angel investors can help their investees is by leveraging their professional networks to help connect investees with venture capitalists who can support their continued development: Wong et al. (n 55) 228. It should, however, be noted that not all financing for earlier stage companies is 'linear', in the sense that angel investment is always necessarily followed by venture capitalist investment. There is evidence that many angel investors are supporting start-ups all the way through to exits, without venture capitalists being involved: *Financing High Growth Firms* (n 52) 19.

[60] Follow-on investments are subsequent rounds of funding to finance a company's continued growth. The fact that venture capitalists tend to have a greater ability to make follow-on investments means that they often dilute an angel's initial investment in a start-up. It has been noted that this adds to an angel's element of risk: Damon (n 52) 45.

[61] Management fees are usually payable every three or six months over the life of the fund and are usually calculated as a percentage of a fund's committed capital (e.g., 2% per annum).

[62] Carried interest payments are often set at around 20% of the profits made on investments. The way in which profits are calculated can differ depending on the arrangement made between venture capitalists and their investors. In some cases, carried interest payments are only paid after capital has been returned to investors together with an additional 'threshold hurdle return', which takes account of the time that the investors' money has been held in the fund.

2.6 Conclusion

This chapter has argued that innovation is vital for economic growth and prosperity and that start-ups play a critical role in a country's innovation system. Venture capital is the 'lifeblood' of many start-ups, and is essential for their survival and growth.[63] It provides start-ups with the vital early stage funding they need to traverse the funding gap known as the 'valley of death'[64] and shift their innovations 'from the laboratory into the factory and on to consumers'.[65] As Terjesen and Frederick have observed, 'if entrepreneurs are the engines that drive new companies, then financing is the fuel that propels them'.[66] Venture capital is, however, highly susceptible to variations in economic conditions and is usually a scarce resource that eludes many start-ups. This makes it all the more important for governments to develop policies that support their countries' venture capital markets. Without dedicated programs that support angel and venture capitalist investment, many countries will fall behind in the highly competitive global innovation race. This will adversely affect not only the growth and productivity of their businesses, but also the living standards of their people. The following chapters build on the discussion in this chapter and examine certain programs that the Australian and United Kingdom Governments have implemented to encourage venture capital investment in their countries' start-ups.

References

Archibugi, Daniele, Jeremy Howells and Jonathan Michie (eds), *Innovation Policy in a Global Economy* (Cambridge University Press, 2003)

Australian Bureau of Statistics, '5678.0 – Venture Capital and Later Stage Private Equity, Australia, 2016–17' (28 February 2018) <http://www.abs.gov.au/AUSSTATS/abs@.nsf/Latestproducts/5678.0Main%20Features12016-17?opendocument&tabname=Summary&prodno=5678.0&issue=2016-17&num=&view=>

Australian Government, *National Innovation and Science Agenda – Welcome to the Ideas Boom* (Report, November 2015)

---

[63] See British Private Equity and Venture Capital Association, *The Rise of Venture Debt in Europe* (Report, May 2010).

[64] The valley of death is a widely used idiomatic expression that can have different meanings in different contexts. For example, one meaning that has been given to the expression is as follows: 'The valley of death describes the point where a business, often a technology based business, has a working prototype for a product or service that has not yet been developed enough to earn money through commercial sales. The company needs to find sufficient money to develop the prototype until it can generate sufficient cash, through sales to customers, that would allow it to be self sufficient and grow': Science and Technology Committee, *Bridging the Valley of Death: Improving the Commercialisation of Research* (Eighth Report of Session 2012–13, House of Commons Science and Technology Committee, 12 March 2013) 8.

[65] Sampsa Samila and Olav Sorenson, 'Venture Capital as a Catalyst to Commercialization' (2010) 39 *Research Policy* 1348, 1349.

[66] Siri Terjesen and Howard Frederick, *Sources of Funding for Australia's Entrepreneurs* (2007) 5.

Australian Government, Department of Industry, Innovation and Science, Office of the Chief Economist, *Australian Innovation System Report 2017* (Report, 2017)

Australian Private Equity and Venture Capital Association Limited, *The Venture Capital Effect: A Report on the Industry's Impact on the Australian Economy* (Report, 13 June 2017)

Banerjee, Chandrajit, 'The Human Factor: The Fundamental Driver of Innovation' in Soumitra Dutta, Bruno Lanvin and Sacha Wunsch-Vincent (eds), *Global Innovation Index 2014 – The Human Factor in Innovation* (Cornell University, INSEAD and WIPO, 2014)

Barkoczy, Stephen, Tamara Wilkinson, Ann Monotti and Mark Davison, *Innovation and Venture Capital Law and Policy* (Federation Press, 2016)

Bartlett, Joseph W, *Fundamentals of Venture Capital* (Madison Books, 1999)

BioCurate <http://www.biocurate.com>

Booth, Bruce, 'Acquisitions as the Silent Partner in Biotech Liquidity: IPO vs. M&A Exit Paths', *Forbes* (online), 27 October 2014 <https://www.forbes.com/sites/brucebooth/2014/10/27/acquisitions-as-the-silent-partner-in-biotech-liquidity-ipo-vs-ma-exit-paths/#727853073561>

British Private Equity and Venture Capital Association, *The Rise of Venture Debt in Europe* (Report, May 2010)

Costello, Sam, *How Many Apps Are in the App Store?* (7 April 2018) Lifewire <https://www.lifewire.com/how-many-apps-in-app-store-2000252>

Cumming, Douglas, 'Introduction' in Douglas Cumming (ed), *The Oxford Handbook of Venture Capital* (Oxford University Press, 2012)

Damon, Dylan Democrat, 'The Legal Aspects of Venture Capital Agreements: Part I' (2007) 25 *Companies and Securities Law Journal* 43

Deschamps, Jean-Philippe, 'Innovation and Leadership' in Larisa V Shavinina (ed), *The International Handbook on Innovation* (Elsevier Science, 2003)

Dogtiev, Artyom, *App Download and Usage Statistics* (8 October 2018) Business of Apps <http://www.businessofapps.com/data/app-statistics/>

Duffy, Jim, 'Zombie Start-ups: Why are Entrepreneurs Failing to Grow their Businesses?' *The Guardian* (online), 7 August 2017 <https://www.theguardian.com/small-business-network/2017/aug/07/zombie-startups-entrepreneurs-failing-grow-businesses>

Dutta, Soumitra, Bruno Lanvin and Sacha Wunsch-Vincent (eds), *Global Innovation Index 2018 – Energizing the World with Innovation* (11th edition, Cornell University, INSEAD and WIPO, 2018)

Fagerberg, Jan, David C Mowery and Richard R Nelson, *The Oxford Handbook of Innovation* (Oxford University Press, 2005)

Ferris, W D, 'Australia Chooses: Venture Capital and a Future Australia' (2001) 26 (Special Issue) *Australian Journal of Management* 45

Goldberg, Itzhak, John Gabriel Goddard, Smita Kuriakose and Jean-Louis Racine, *Igniting Innovation – Rethinking the Role of Government in Emerging Europe and Central Asia* (Report, World Bank, 2011)

Golis, Christopher C, Patrick D Mooney and Thomas F Richardson, *Enterprise and Venture Capital: A Business Builders' and Investors' Handbook* (Allen and Unwin, 5th ed, 2009)

Greenhalgh, Christine and Mark Rogers, *Innovation, Intellectual Property, and Economic Growth* (Princeton University Press, 2010)

Gruener, A and R Kutz, 'Trade Sale versus IPO as Exit Strategy – An Empirical Analysis of European and US VC Backed Biotechnology Companies' (2017) 1(4) *Austin Journal of Business Administration and Management* 1

Hall, Bronwyn H and Nathan Rosenberg (eds), *Handbook of the Economics of Innovation: Volumes 1 and 2* (Elsevier, 2010)

Hogg, Sam, 'Zombie VC Firms Can Be an Entrepreneur's Nightmare', *Entrepreneur* (online), 31 October 2013 <https://www.entrepreneur.com/article/227925>

HM Treasury and the Department for Business Innovation & Skills, 'Our Plan for Growth: Science and Innovation' (December 2014)

Hyndman, James, *Let's Stop Using the Word 'Innovation'* (9 April 2018) Quinn Allan <https://www.quinnallan.com.au/market-news-item/lets-stop-using-word-innovation/>

Innovation and Science Australia, *Australia 2030: Prosperity Through Innovation* (Report, November 2017)

Johnson, Calvin H, 'Why Do Venture Capital Funds Burn Research and Development Deductions' (2009) 29(1) *Virginia Tax Review* 29

King, Agnes and Caitlin Fitzsimmons, 'How the Mathematics of Venture Capital Has Changed and What it Means for Start-Up Exits', *Australian Financial Review* (online), 18 March 2015 <https://www.afr.com/it-pro/how-the-mathematics-of-venture-capital-has-changed-and-what-it-means-for-startup-exits-20150318-1m22dq>

Microsoft, 'Best Practices for Innovation: Microsoft's Innovation Management Framework' (Microsoft Corporation, June 2013)

Nelson, Richard R, *The Sources of Economic Growth* (Harvard University Press, 2000)

OECD, *Financing High-Growth Firms – The Role of Angel Investors* (OECD, 2011)

OECD, *Main Science and Technology Indicators* (2017) <https://stats.oecd.org/Index.aspx?DataSetCode=MSTI_PUB>

OECD, *OSLO Manual: Guidelines for Collecting and Interpreting Innovation Data* (OECD, 3rd ed, 2005)

OECD, *Science, Technology and Industry Scoreboard 2009* (OECD, 2009)

Powell, Dominic, 'Sydney Angels Reveals Investment Data: 54 Startups Have Received $193 Million Since 2008', *Smart Company*, 18 December 2017 <https://www.smartcompany.com.au/startupsmart/news-analysis/sydney-angels-reveals-investment-data/>

Productivity Commission, *Business Set-up, Transfer and Closure* (Report No 75, Productivity Commission, 30 September 2015)

Rainey, David L, *Product Innovation: Leading Change through Integrated Product Development* (Cambridge University Press, 2005)

Samila, Sampsa and Olav Sorenson, 'Venture Capital as a Catalyst to Commercialization' (2010) 39 *Research Policy* 1348

Science and Technology Committee, *Bridging the Valley of Death: Improving the Commercialisation of Research* (Eighth Report of Session 2012–13, House of Commons Science and Technology Committee, 12 March 2013)

Senate Economics References Committee, *Access of Small Business to Finance* (Report, 30 June 2010)

Shah, Sohin, 'How Disruptive Startups Spread the Wealth by Encouraging Derivative Businesses', *Entrepreneur* (online), 3 June 2015 <http://www.entrepreneur.com/article/246783>

Spillman, John H, 'United States of America' in Beat A Brechbühl and Bob Wooder (eds), *Global Venture Capital Transactions: A Practical Approach* (Kluwer Law International, 2004)

StartupAUS, *Crossroads 2015 – An Action Plan to Develop a Vibrant Tech Startup Ecosystem in Australia* (Report, 2015)

StartupAUS, *Crossroads – An Action Plan to Develop a Vibrant Tech Startup Ecosystem in Australia* (Report, 2016)

StartupAUS, *Crossroads: An Action Plan to Develop a World-Leading Tech Startup Ecosystem in Australia* (Report, 2017)

Tadros, Edmund, 'Innovation a Mere Buzzword for More Than Half of Firms', *Australian Financial Review* (online), 27 June 2017 <https://www.afr.com/business/accounting/innovation-a-mere-buzzword-for-more-than-half-of-firms-20170625-gwyabb>

Tantry, Sathvik, *How Venture Capital Incentives Promote Zombie Companies* (7 August 2015) TechCrunch <https://techcrunch.com/2015/08/06/how-venture-capital-incentives-promote-zombie-companies/>

Terjesen, Siri and Howard Frederick, *Sources of Funding for Australia's Entrepreneurs* (2007)

Times Higher Education, *World University Rankings 2018* (2018) <https://www.timeshighereducation.com/world-university-rankings/2018/world-ranking#!/page/0/length/100/sort_by/scores_overall/sort_order/asc/cols/scores>

Treasury and Department of Industry, Innovation, Science, Research and Tertiary Education, *Review of Venture Capital and Entrepreneurial Skills* (Final Report, 2012)

Universities Australia, 'Keep it Clever' (Policy Statement 2016, 7 October 2015)

Utterback, James M, *Mastering the Dynamics of Innovation* (Harvard Business School Press, 1994)

Williams, Ross, Anne Leahy, Gaétan de Rassenfosse and Paul Jensen, *U21 Ranking of National Higher Education Systems 2015* (Report, Melbourne Institute of Applied Economic and Social Research, May 2015)

Wong, Andrew, Mihir Bhatia and Zachary Freeman, 'Angel Finance: The Other Venture Capital' (2009) 18 *Strategic Change* 221

World Bank, *Innovation Policy – A Guide for Developing Countries* (World Bank, 2010)

Yin, Pai-Ling, Jason P Davis and Yulia Muzyrya, 'Entrepreneurial Innovation: Killer Apps in the iPhone Ecosystem' (2014) 104(5) *American Economic Review* 255

Chapter 3
Australia's Formal Venture Capital Tax Incentive Programs

Abstract One of the common ways that governments support their countries' innovation systems is by introducing special tax incentives to encourage venture capital investment in start-ups. Designing venture capital tax incentive programs is a complex task that involves a range of different policy considerations. One of these considerations is deciding whether to provide investors with front-end or back-end incentives in relation to their investments. Front end incentives are usually provided by way of deductions and tax offsets in the income year in which an investment is made, while back-end incentives are usually provided in the form of income tax and capital gains tax exemptions in the income year in which investments are disposed of. While front-end incentives provide an immediate benefit to investors, back-end incentives may be preferable from a government's perspective, as they are deferred and generally only arise in relation to financially successful investments. Over the years, the Australian Government has introduced a number of intricate tax incentive programs to encourage formal venture capital investment. These programs have evolved considerably over time and have provided investors with a range of front-end and back-end tax incentives in relation to their investments in specially licensed and registered venture capital funds. The earlier programs (the Management and Investment Companies program and the Pooled Development Funds program) provide tax incentives for investments made through companies, while the more recent programs (the Venture Capital Limited Partnership program and the Early Stage Venture Capital Limited Partnership program) provide tax incentives for investments made through limited partnerships. This chapter discusses the key features of Australia's formal venture capital tax incentive programs. The programs are then compared and contrasted with the angel tax incentives provided under the ESI program and the SEIS in the following chapters.

S. Barkoczy, T. Wilkinson, *Incentivising Angels*, SpringerBriefs in Law,
https://doi.org/10.1007/978-981-13-6632-1_3

3.1 Introduction

As discussed in Chap. 1, in order to support their innovation systems, many governments around the world have designed special programs to encourage venture capital investment in their countries' start-ups. One of the main ways that governments have sought to stimulate venture capital activity is by providing tax incentives to venture capital investors. In designing their venture capital tax incentive programs, governments need to consider a broad range of factors, including who will benefit under such programs, how much they will cost in terms of foregone revenue and whether there should be any monetary caps or other restrictions on the amount of incentives taxpayers may claim. Governments need to be careful in setting the criteria for the kinds of investments they are seeking to promote and the kinds of entities in which they wish investments to be made. In particular, they need to consider whether the tax incentives are available for angel and/or formal venture capital investment, and whether the start-ups in which investments are made must be of a particular size or stage of development or involved in any special industries.

Governments have the choice of providing venture capital tax incentives at the time an investment is made ('front-end incentives'), or when the investment is subsequently realised or disposed of ('back-end incentives'). Front-end incentives are usually provided to investors in the form of 'deductions'[1] or 'tax offsets'[2] in the income year in which they make their investments. Back-end incentives, on the other hand, are generally provided to investors in the form of exemptions from income tax and CGT in the income year in which they exit their investments. While front-end incentives provide investors with immediate benefits irrespective of how their investments ultimately perform, back-end incentives generally only arise in relation to financially successful investments, as it is only those investments that have generated a profit or gain which would otherwise suffer tax when they are disposed of. From a government's perspective, one of the advantages of back-end

[1] Under Australia's income tax laws, taxpayers subtract their deductions from their 'assessable income' to arrive at their taxable income for an income year: ITAA 1997 s 4-15. A taxpayer's taxable income is the amount upon which they must pay income tax. Different taxpayers pay different rates of tax. For example, an individual pays tax at progressive marginal rates of up to 45% (plus a 2% Medicare levy), while a company generally pays tax at a flat rate of 27.5% (if it is a 'base rate entity') or 30% (in other cases). Ultimately, the benefit of a tax deduction to a taxpayer is a function of their respective tax rate. As a $1 deduction reduces a taxpayer's taxable income by $1, it results in the taxpayer paying an amount of $1 multiplied by their respective tax rate less in tax.

[2] Under Australia's income tax laws, tax offsets are subtracted from the tax payable on a taxpayer's taxable income: ITAA 1997 s 4-10. The benefit of a tax offset is therefore not a function of the taxpayer's tax rate, as is the case with a deduction (see n 1). A $1 tax offset reduces a taxpayer's tax payable by a full $1. Some tax offsets are refundable, whereas others are not refundable: Division 67. If a tax offset is refundable, so much of the tax offset which exceeds the tax payable on the taxpayer's taxable income is refunded to the taxpayer. If the tax offset is not refundable, the amount of any excess tax offset is generally lost. Special carry forward rules allow certain non-refundable tax offsets that have not been fully utilised in an income year to be carried forward into future years: Division 65. The ESVCLP tax offset discussed at [3.4] and the ESI tax offset discussed at [4.3] are examples of non-refundable tax offsets that may be carried forward: s 63-10.

incentives is that their cost is deferred until such time that the investments prove to be successful. This also makes it easier for the government to justify the incentives to voters on the basis that it is 'backing winners'. Another advantage of back-end incentives is that they allow the government to indirectly recoup the cost of providing the incentives to investors through the taxes collected from the successful investee companies that have benefited from funding under the relevant program.[3]

3.2 Australia's Formal Venture Capital Tax Incentive Programs

The Australian Government has been using tax incentives to encourage venture capital investment since long before the introduction of the ESI program in 2016. While the Government has not previously provided any angel tax incentives, it has relied heavily on tax incentives to develop the formal venture capital market in Australia. Over the last 35 years, the Government has established four formal venture capital tax incentive programs. These programs are known as:

- the Management and Investment Companies (MIC) program;
- the Pooled Development Funds (PDF) program;
- the Venture Capital Limited Partnership (VCLP) program; and
- the Early Stage Venture Capital Limited Partnership (ESVCLP) program.

The programs are complex and are heavily regulated under various pieces of legislation.[4] They provide a range of front-end and back-end tax incentives to investors who invest in special types of regulated venture capital funds. These funds must be licensed or registered by the relevant regulator, which is currently ISA.[5] As will be discussed further below, the respective programs use different kinds of investment vehicles for making venture capital investments. The first two programs use companies to operate as venture capital funds, whereas the last two programs use limited partnerships to operate as venture capital funds. This means that the ultimate investors in the first two programs are the shareholders in the relevant companies, whereas the investors in the last two programs are the partners in the relevant partnerships. It is important to understand that the first program was terminated in 1991 and the second program was closed to new registrants in 2007. The third and fourth programs are fully active and operate alongside the ESI program.

---

[3] Stephen Barkoczy, Tamara Wilkinson, Ann Monotti and Mark Davison, *Innovation and Venture Capital Law and Policy* (Federation Press, 2016) 125.

[4] The key Acts governing the respective programs are the former *Management and Investment Companies Act* 1983 (Cth) ('MIC Act'), the *Pooled Development Funds Act* 1992 (Cth) ('PDF Act'), the *Venture Capital Act* 2002 (Cth) ('VC Act'), the *Income Tax Assessment Act* 1936 (Cth) ('ITAA 1936') and the ITAA 1997.

[5] Former regulators include the MIC Licensing Board and the PDF Registration Board.

Although the principal focus of this book is on angel tax incentives, it is useful to examine some of the key features of Australia's formal venture capital tax incentive programs in order to better understand the historical context behind the introduction of the ESI program and the relationships that exist between the relevant programs. The following discussion examines some of the key features of Australia's formal venture capital tax incentive programs.[6]

3.3 MIC and PDF Programs

Australia's first formal venture capital tax incentive program was the Management and Investment Companies ('MIC') program, which commenced its operation in 1983.[7] The MIC program allowed companies that were licensed as MICs to invest in 'eligible business entities'[8] and certain other approved investments.[9] Broadly speaking, eligible business entities were business entities that had not more than 100 employees or a net worth of not more than $6 million, were involved in specific kinds of business activities, and had expected sales growth of 20% over 3 years.[10] To encourage participation in the MIC program, taxpayers who subscribed for shares in MICs were provided with front-end incentives in the form of tax deductions for

[6] As Australia's formal venture capital tax incentive programs are complex, it is not possible to discuss all of their intricate features in a book of this nature. For a detailed analysis of the programs, see Barkoczy et al. (n 3) 278–338; Stephen Barkoczy and Daniel Sandler, *Government Venture Capital Incentives: A Multi-Jurisdiction Comparative Analysis* (Australian Tax Research Foundation, 2007); Stephen Barkoczy, Don Maloney and Wayne Ngo, *Pooled Development Funds Handbook* (Australian Tax Practice, 2001).

[7] The origins of the MIC program can be traced to recommendations contained in a report (commonly referred to as the 'Espie report') which indicated that Australia did not have a venture capital market at the time: Australian Academy of Technological Sciences, *High Technology Financing Committee, Developing High Technology Enterprises for Australia* (Report, 1983).

[8] MIC Act s 29.

[9] MIC Act s 37. The MIC Licensing Board could approve a range of investments, including loans to or deposits with banks and dealers in the short-term money market. Permitting MICs to make these kinds of investments allowed them to park their capital while searching for investments in eligible business entities.

[10] A business entity was defined as a company, partnership, unit trust or sole trader: MIC Act s 3. The business entity had to be certified by the MIC Licensing Board and had to be engaged primarily in one the following business activities: manufacturing; prescribed agricultural, forestry or fishing activities; postal, telegraphic, telephonic or teleprinter communication services or such other communication services as prescribed; architectural services; surveying services; the production or supply of software for computers or for similar equipment; consultant engineering services; scientific and technical services; data processing services; or prescribed services relating to education or training: s 29. An MIC could not invest more than 20% of its approved capital or shareholders' funds (whichever was greater) in a particular eligible business entity: s 32. An MIC could hold up to 50%, or such higher amount as the MIC Licensing Board approved, of the ownership interests in a business entity: s 33.

the amounts they paid to purchase their shares.[11] Although the MIC program kick-started the formal venture capital industry in Australia,[12] it was a 'clunky' regime that was criticised for having a high degree of regulation and problematic investment rules.[13] As a result, it was eventually terminated in 1991.

The MIC program was succeeded by the PDF program, which was introduced in 1992. While the PDF program has some broad structural similarities with the MIC program, it also has a number of significant differences. The PDF program allowed companies to apply to become registered as PDFs.[14] Like MICs, PDFs raise capital by issuing shares to their shareholders.[15] To ensure that PDFs operate as pooled investment vehicles, a person together with their associates is generally prevented from holding more than 30% of the issued shares in a PDF.[16] The PDF legislation requires PDFs to use their capital to carry on a business of making and holding 'PDF investments'.[17] The main form of PDF investment is commonly known as an 'SME investment'. PDFs are allowed to buy shares,[18] acquire non-transferable options to buy shares[19] or lend money[20] to companies[21] with assets not exceeding $50 million.[22] These companies must generally not have as their primary activity an excluded activity (i.e., retail sale operations, and acquisitions and disposals of

---

[11] ITAA 1936 former s 77F. The deductions operated subject to 'claw-back rules', under which they were either fully or partially withdrawn if an investor's shares were disposed of within a period of 4 years.

[12] Over the life of the program, a total of 14 MICs raised $374 million of capital, of which $225.45 million was invested in 155 businesses: Management and Investment Companies Licensing Board, *Annual Report 1990–91* (Report, 1991) 2. See also OECD, *Government Venture Capital for Technology-Based Firms* (Report, 1997) 29.

[13] Barkoczy et al. (n 3) 287–8.

[14] PDF Act ss 10-18.

[15] Issuing shares is the principal way in which PDFs raise capital, as they are generally not permitted to borrow money: PDF Act s 30.

[16] PDF Act s 31. Note that ISA can approve a person to hold more than 30% of the shares in a PDF In addition, the 30% rule does not apply to certain entities, such as banks, life offices and widely-held complying superannuation funds.

[17] PDF Act ss 19, 29. PDF investments are defined as investments permitted under Division 1 of Part 4 of the PDF Act: s 4.

[18] PDF Act s 20. Unless ISA otherwise approves the shares must not be pre-owned shares.

[19] PDF Act s 20A.

[20] PDF Act s 20B. Unless ISA approves, a PDF cannot lend money to a company unless it first holds shares in the company and the total of all amounts paid on those shares is at least 10% of all amounts paid on the issued shares in the company: s 27.

[21] The companies must have share capital and be incorporated in Australia, or taken to be incorporated, under the *Corporations Act* 2001 (Cth): PDF Act s 4. This ensures that such companies are effectively Australian companies.

[22] PDF Act s 24. There is a general requirement that, at the time of making an investment in a company, a PDF must believe on reasonable grounds that the investment is made solely or principally for the purpose of establishing an eligible business to be carried on by the investee company or substantially expanding its production capacity or markets: s 21.

interests in, or the development of, land).[23] In addition to making SME investments, PDFs are also permitted to make 'unregulated investments' which cover certain bank investments (e.g., loans and deposits) and investments in the short-term money market.[24] The purpose of allowing PDFs to make unregulated investments is to enable them to 'park' their capital while they search for SME investments.[25] To ensure that PDFs focus on making SME investments, they are required to invest at least 65% of their capital in eligible companies within 5 years.[26]

Under the PDF program, shareholders do not obtain a front-end deduction for purchasing shares in a PDF as was the case for purchasing shares in an MIC under the MIC program. Instead, to encourage investment in PDFs, shareholders are provided with back-end incentives in the form of exemptions from income tax and CGT when they subsequently dispose of their PDF shares.[27] The change from front-end incentives under the MIC program to back-end incentives under the PDF program is a key difference between the architecture of the programs. Another important difference is that PDFs are taxed at concessional rates[28] and dividends paid by PDFs are generally exempt from tax in the hands of their shareholders.[29] MICs, on the other hand, paid tax at the general corporate tax rate and their dividends were taxable.

Although the PDF program remains in existence today, its scope has been steadily shrinking as it has not been possible to register any new PDFs since 21 June 2007. This is due to the introduction of the ESVCLP program (discussed below), which was specifically designed to supersede the PDF program. Although the PDF program has therefore been 'frozen', the tax incentives available under the program nevertheless continue to apply to all remaining PDFs and their shareholders.[30]

---

[23] PDF Act s 23; Pooled Development Funds Regulations 2018 (Cth) reg 6. Retail sale and land development activities are excluded presumably because companies engaged in these activities are not generally viewed in the same light as start-ups. Companies engaged in retail sale and land development activities are not usually considered to be innovative or high-risk in the same way as start-ups, and they do not usually struggle to obtain finance in the same way as start-ups. Note that ISA may, in certain cases, approve an excluded activity.

[24] PDF Act s 4(1); Pooled Development Funds Regulations 2018 (Cth) reg 7.

[25] In this regard, the provision has a similar function to s 37 of the MIC Act (see n 9).

[26] PDF Act s 32.

[27] ITAA 1936 s 124ZN; ITAA 1997 s 118-13. It is worth noting that shareholders are exempt from income tax and CGT on both their gains and losses from the disposal of their PDF shares. The 'symmetrical' feature of the exemptions means that they operate as a 'double-edged sword': see further Barkoczy et al. (n 3) 296.

[28] PDFs pay tax at the rate of 15% on the 'SME income component' of their taxable income and 25% on the 'unregulated investment component' of their taxable income. Broadly speaking, the SME income component of a PDF's taxable income is so much of its taxable income that relates to its investments in eligible investee companies, while the unregulated investment component of its taxable income is so much of its taxable income that relates to its unregulated investments (e.g., income from bank deposits): *Income Tax Rates Act* 1986 (Cth) s 23(5).

[29] ITAA 1997s 124ZM. Shareholders can also elect to be taxed on PDF dividends, in which case, they are eligible to benefit from the franking credits allocated to the dividends.

[30] As at February 2018, there were still 23 registered PDFs: Department of Industry, Innovation and Science, 'Companies Registered as Pooled Development Funds' (February 2018).

3.4 VCLP and ESVCLP Programs

Most formal venture capital investment in Australia nowadays takes place under the VCLP and ESVCLP programs. These two programs are closely related to each other and have a substantial number of overlapping provisions. They are, however, quite different programs with their own distinct policy objectives. The VCLP program was introduced in 2002 with the aim of encouraging international venture capital investment in Australia from foreign entities. The ESVCLP program, on the other hand, was introduced in 2007 to replace the PDF program, and focuses primarily on encouraging domestic venture capital investment.

Both programs use special limited partnership investment vehicles, known as VCLPs and ESVCLPs, to make investments. These vehicles are usually established as 'incorporated limited partnerships'[31] and are required to be registered with ISA and operate as regulated venture capital funds.[32] The reason for switching from corporate investment vehicles (as used under the MIC and PDF programs) to limited partnership investment vehicles is that limited partnerships are widely used internationally, particularly in the United States, for venture capital investment.[33] The use of these vehicles therefore makes Australia's venture capital funds more familiar to international investors. Another special feature of VCLPs and ESVCLPs is that, unlike companies, they are taxed on a 'transparent' basis.[34] As a result, any gains and losses made on their investments automatically 'flow through' to the respective partners in accordance with their interests in the partnership.

VCLPs and ESVCLPs are managed by their 'general partners' (who are the venture capitalists) and raise capital from their 'limited partners' (who are the investors). VCLPs and ESVCLPs are required to use their capital to make 'eligible

---

[31] Incorporated limited partnerships are a special form of limited partnership that have been specifically designed for use under the VCLP and ESVCLP programs. Like other limited partnerships, an incorporated limited partnership has both 'general partners' (who manage the partnership) and 'limited partners' (who invest in the partnership). An incorporated limited partnership is, however, a body corporate which has a distinct legal personality (like a company) which is separate from both its general and limited partners. Incorporated limited partnerships are established under relevant State and Territory legislation: see *Partnership Act* 1892 (NSW) Part 3; *Partnership Act* 1891 (Qld) Chap. 4; *Partnership Act* 1891 (SA) Part 3; *Partnership Act* 1891 (Tas) Part 3; *Partnership Act* 1958 (Vic) Part 5; *Partnership Act* 1963 (ACT); Part 6; *Partnership Act* 1997 (NT) Part 3.

[32] VC Act Divisions 9–15.

[33] For further details relating to the reasons behind the use of the limited partnership model under the VCLP and ESVCLP programs, see Miranda Stewart, 'Venture Capital Tax Reform in Australia and New Zealand' (2005) 11 *New Zealand Journal of Taxation Law and Policy* 216; Keith Fletcher, 'Incorporated Limited Partnerships: Venture Capital's Contribution to Legal Development' (2004) 17 *Australian Journal of Corporate Law* 157; AVCAL, Gilbert + Tobin and Freehills, 'Venture Capital Limited Partnerships – Proposed Amendments to State and Territory Partnership Statutes to Develop a World Best Practice Venture Capital Investment Structure' (Revised Submission, 24 April 2003).

[34] ITAA 1997 Division 5 of Part III.

venture capital investments'.[35] An eligible venture capital investment is, broadly speaking, an investment consisting of an acquisition of shares, options or convertible notes in a company or unit trust that are held 'at risk'[36] and meet a number of complex technical requirements, including special 'location within Australia' and 'predominant activity' requirements.[37]

The location within Australia requirements require the company or trust to meet certain residency related requirements.[38] In addition, if, at the time of making the investment, the investor does not own any other investments in the company or trust, the company or trust must have (unless ISA determines otherwise) more than 50% of its assets (determined by value) situated in Australia, and more than 50% of its service performers performing those services primarily in Australia, during the 12 months (or such shorter period as ISA allows) from the time the investment is made.[39]

The predominant activity requirements require the company or unit trust to satisfy at least two of the following requirements:

- more than 75% of the assets of the company or trust or their controlled entities must be used primarily in activities that are not ineligible activities;
- more than 75% of the employees of the company or trust or their controlled entities must be engaged primarily in activities that are not ineligible activities;
- more than 75% of the total income of the company or trust and their controlled entities must come from activities that are not ineligible activities.[40]

The concept of ineligible activities is wider than the concept of excluded activities under the PDF program. Ineligible activities include: property development or land ownership; finance (to the extent that it involves banking, providing capital to others, leasing, factoring or securitisation); insurance; construction or acquisition of infrastructure or related facilities; and making investments directed at deriving interest, rent, dividends, royalties or lease payments.[41]

---

[35] ITAA 1997 ss 118-425, 118-427.

[36] ITAA 1997 s 118-430. An eligible venture capital investment is at-risk if the entity that owns the investment has no arrangement as to the maintenance of the value of the investment or any earnings or other return that might be made from owning the investment.

[37] ITAA 1997 ss 118-425(1), 118-427(1).

[38] If the investment is in a company, the company must, at the time the investment is made, be an Australian resident: ITAA 1997 s 118-425(2). If the investment is in a unit trust, the unit trust must, at the time the investment is made, carry on business in Australia, and either have its central management and control in Australia or have more than 50% of the beneficial interests in its income or property held by Australian residents: s 118-427(3).

[39] A special rule allows investments to be made in companies or unit trusts that do not satisfy these requirements if the total of such investments does not exceed 20% of the VCLP's or ESVCLP's committed capital: ITAA 1997 ss 118-425(12A), 118-427(13).

[40] ITAA 1997 ss 118-425(3), 118-427(4)

[41] ITAA 1997 ss 118-425(13), 118-427(14). However, note that activities that consist of developing technology (or that are ancillary to incidental to developing technology) in relation to finance, insurance or making investments are not ineligible activities: ss 118-425(13A), 118-427(14A).

One of the key differences between the VCLP and ESVCLP programs is that VCLPs are allowed to invest in qualifying companies and unit trusts valued at up to $250 million, whereas ESVCLPs are only allowed to invest in qualifying companies and unit trusts valued at up to $50 million.[42] Another difference between the VCLP and ESVCLP programs is that while VCLPs are generally free to invest in pre-owned shares and units, ESVCLPs can only make pre-owned investments in limited circumstances, and their investment plans generally require them to focus on early stage venture capital investments.[43] The ESVCLP program is therefore a much 'purer' venture capital program than the VCLP program, which extends well beyond venture capital investment to the broader class of private equity investment.

A further difference between the VCLP and ESVCLP programs is that the ESVCLP program contains a special requirement that a partner's committed capital in an ESVCLP (together with the committed capital of their associates) must generally not exceed 30% of the partnership's committed capital.[44] This rule performs a similar function to the 30% issued share rule under the PDF program (see 3.3).[45] It is designed to ensure that ESVCLPs ordinarily operate as pooled investment vehicles with a minimum of four unassociated partners. There is no similar requirement under the VCLP program.

As the VCLP program was introduced specifically to attract international investment, the tax incentives provided under the program are only available to certain categories of foreign investors.[46] In contrast, the ESVCLP program provides tax incentives to both domestic and foreign investors.[47] Under both programs, eligible

Likewise, an activity relating to finance, insurance or making investments that is covered by a private or public finding from ISA under s 118-432 stating that it is a substantially novel application of technology is not an ineligible activity.

[42] The $50 million value prescribed under the ESVCLP program corresponds with the $50 million value prescribed under the PDF program. Note, however, that under the ESVCLP program investments can be made in both companies and unit trusts, whereas under the PDF program investments must be made in companies.

[43] VC Act ss 13(1A), 13-20.

[44] VC Act s 9-3(1)(e). There are some limited exceptions to this rule. In particular, it does not apply to certain investors (such as banks, life insurance companies and widely-held superannuation funds), or where ISA allows a partner's committed capital to exceed the 30% limit: ss 9-3(4), (5), 9-4.

[45] PDF Act s 31.

[46] More specifically, the tax incentives are only available to a VCLP's 'eligible venture capital partners': ITAA 1997 s 118-405. These partners fall within four categories: (i) tax-exempt foreign residents; (ii) foreign venture capital funds of funds whose committed capital in the partnership does not exceed 30% of the partnership's total committed capital; (iii) widely held foreign venture capital fund of funds; and (iv) foreign residents who are not general partners of a VCLP or ESVCLP and are neither tax exempt foreign residents or widely held foreign venture capital fund of funds and whose committed capital (together with the committed capital of any connected entities) in the partnership is less than 10% of the partnership's total committed capital: s 118-420.

[47] While all limited partners (whether Australian residents or foreign residents) in an ESVCLP are eligible for the tax incentives, the general partners only qualify for the tax incentives if they are Australian residents or residents of a country with which Australia has a double tax agreement: ITAA 1997 s 118-407.

investors receive back-end incentives in the form of income tax and CGT exemptions on their respective shares of any gains and losses made by a fund on its eligible venture capital investments.[48]

Investors in ESVCLPs also receive income tax exemptions on any income derived from eligible venture capital investments (such as dividends).[49] In addition, from 1 July 2016, a new front-end incentive in the form of a 10% tax offset has become available to limited partners that contribute capital to ESVCLPs.[50] This incentive is designed to further bolster investment in the ESVCLP program and, like the ESI program, was announced as part of NISA.

A special feature of the VCLP and ESVCLP programs is that the general partners are taxed under the CGT rules in respect of their carried interest payments.[51] Carried interest payments are therefore not assessable as ordinary income.[52] Taxing carried interest payments under the CGT regime enables the general partners to reduce the amount of the capital gains generated on their carried interest payments by a CGT discount of 50%, provided they meet certain criteria.[53] The purpose behind the special CGT treatment of carried interest payments is to encourage fund managers to establish VCLPs and ESVCLPs and therefore hopefully broaden the pool of venture capital available for investment in start-ups. There was no similar incentive available to the managers of MICs or PDFs for performance bonuses paid under either the MIC or PDF programs.

3.5 Conclusion

This chapter has shown that Australia's formal venture capital tax incentive programs are complex and have evolved considerably over the years. As can be seen from the preceding discussion, these programs provide a broad range of front-end and back-end tax incentives. It is important to understand the key features of the programs, particularly the more recent programs, being the VCLP and ESVCLP programs, as they operate closely alongside the ESI program. The following chapter examines the ESI program in detail and compares and contrasts various aspects of it with aspects of the formal venture capital tax incentive programs discussed in this chapter.

---

[48] ITAA 1997 ss 26-68, 51-54, 118-405, 118-407, 118-425, 118-427. As the exemptions available to eligible investors in VCLPs and ESVCLPs apply to their shares of any relevant gains or losses on eligible venture capital investments, the exemptions operate as a double-edged sword in much the same way that the exemptions apply to shareholders in PDFs on the disposal of their PDF shares (see n 27).

[49] ITAA 1997 s 51-52.

[50] ITAA 1997 ss 61-760, 61-765. As mentioned above (n 2), this tax offset is a non-refundable tax offset that may be carried forward to later income years under the special rules in Division 65: s 63-10.

[51] ITAA 1997 s 104-255.

[52] ITAA 1997 s 118-21

[53] ITAA 1997 Division 115.

References

Australian Academy of Technological Sciences, *High Technology Financing Committee, Developing High Technology Enterprises for Australia* (Report, 1983)

AVCAL, Gilbert + Tobin and Freehills, 'Venture Capital Limited Partnerships – Proposed Amendments to State and Territory Partnership Statutes to Develop a World Best Practice Venture Capital Investment Structure' (Revised Submission, 24 April 2003)

Barkoczy, Stephen and Daniel Sandler, *Government Venture Capital Incentives: A Multi-Jurisdiction Comparative Analysis* (Australian Tax Research Foundation, 2007)

Barkoczy, Stephen, Don Maloney and Wayne Ngo, *Pooled Development Funds Handbook* (Australian Tax Practice, 2001)

Barkoczy, Stephen, Tamara Wilkinson, Ann Monotti and Mark Davison, *Innovation and Venture Capital Law and Policy* (Federation Press, 2016)

Corporations Act 2001 (Cth)

Department of Industry, Innovation and Science, 'Companies Registered as Pooled Development Funds' (February 2018)

Fletcher, Keith 'Incorporated Limited Partnerships: Venture Capital's Contribution to Legal Development' (2004) 17 *Australian Journal of Corporate Law* 157

Income Tax Assessment Act 1936 (Cth)

Income Tax Assessment Act 1997 (Cth)

Income Tax Rates Act 1986 (Cth)

Management and Investment Companies Act 1983 (Cth)

Management and Investment Companies Licensing Board, *Annual Report 1990–91* (Report, 1991)

OECD, *Government Venture Capital for Technology-Based Firms* (Report, 1997)

Partnership Act 1891 (Qld)

Partnership Act 1891 (SA)

Partnership Act 1891 (Tas)

Partnership Act 1892 (NSW)

Partnership Act 1958 (Vic)

Partnership Act 1963 (ACT)

Partnership Act 1997 (NT)

Pooled Development Funds Act 1992 (Cth)

Pooled Development Funds Regulations 2018 (Cth)

Stewart, Miranda 'Venture Capital Tax Reform in Australia and New Zealand' (2005) 11 *New Zealand Journal of Taxation Law and Policy* 216

Venture Capital Act 2002 (Cth)

Chapter 4
Australia's Early Stage Investor Program

Abstract Australia's ESI program is a revolutionary new tax incentive program designed to stimulate venture capital investment in eligible start-ups, known as 'early stage innovation companies' (ESICs). The ESI program operates alongside Australia's other venture capital tax incentive programs discussed in Chap. 3. Whereas these other programs focus on encouraging venture capital investment made indirectly by investors through regulated venture capital funds run by venture capitalists, the ESI program is targeted at venture capital investment made directly by angel investors. The ESI program offers generous front-end and back-end tax incentives to encourage investors to subscribe for shares in ESICs. Eligible investors can generally claim a front-end 20% tax offset (capped at $200,000 per year) on their investment in an ESIC. In addition, they are also deemed to hold their shares on capital account and entitled to modified CGT treatment when they exit their investments, including a back-end exemption on capital gains made from any CGT event in relation to shares that they have continuously held for at least one year and less than 10 years since their issue. The ESI program is quite complex and requires a range of intricate criteria to be satisfied in order for investors to be eligible to claim the tax incentives. This chapter explains the policy rationale behind the introduction of the ESI program and discusses its technical requirements in detail. Special attention is devoted to the program's 'early stage' and 'innovation' requirements, which are crucial for determining whether a start-up qualifies as an ESIC. The tax incentives available under the program are also closely scrutinised and evaluated.

S. Barkoczy, T. Wilkinson, *Incentivising Angels*, SpringerBriefs in Law,
https://doi.org/10.1007/978-981-13-6632-1_4

4.1 Background

As discussed in Chap. 1, the ESI program is contained in Subdivision 360-A of the ITAA 1997 and provides tax incentives to encourage informal venture capital investment by angel investors.[1] The ESI program is therefore very different from the tax incentive programs discussed in Chap. 3, which are all focused on encouraging formal venture capital investment through regulated funds run by venture capitalists. While Australia's formal venture capital tax incentive programs have been around for many years, the ESI program has only been in existence for just over 2 years and is the Australian Government's first angel tax incentive program. It therefore constitutes a significant new policy initiative that warrants close analysis.

The ESI program uses a combination of front-end and back-end tax incentives to encourage investors to subscribe for shares in early stage innovation companies (ESICs). As will be discussed below, an ESIC is a company that meets certain 'early stage' and 'innovation' requirements (see 4.2). Eligible investors are entitled to a capped, non-refundable tax offset in the income year in which they make their investments in an ESIC (see 4.3). In addition, they are also deemed to hold their shares on capital account and are subject to modified CGT treatment, including an exemption from CGT on capital gains made from any CGT event in relation to shares that they have continuously held for at least one year and less than 10 years since their issue (see 4.4).

The Explanatory Memorandum to the Bill that introduced the ESI program explains that the program is designed to promote an entrepreneurial culture by connecting investors with start-ups, particularly those in the seed and pre-commercialisation phases.[2] The risks associated with investing at these early stages are extremely high, and it is unusual for a company to receive significant amounts of formal venture capital funding at this point.[3] From a policy perspective, the Government is therefore seeking to encourage investment in those companies that are generally unlikely to benefit greatly from its formal venture capital tax incentive programs.[4] In other words, it is trying to address a specific market failure. As the Explanatory Memorandum states, the aim of the ESI program is to 'bridge the funding gap between pre-concept stage financing … and financing through the ESVCLP and VCLP regimes for companies further along the development pathway'.[5]

---

[1] While the ESI program does not specifically refer to 'angels', it is clear from the type of investments permitted under the program that the incentive is directed principally towards these investors. However, as will be revealed below, other kinds of investors that do not necessarily fall within the classic definition of angels (e.g., companies) may also be eligible for the incentives.

[2] Explanatory Memorandum, Tax Laws Amendment (Tax Incentives for Innovation) Bill 2016 (Cth) 1.4, 1.6 ('*ESI Explanatory Memorandum*').

[3] As the *ESI Explanatory Memorandum* notes, 'venture capital funds typically focus on companies that have already developed a concept that is anticipated to attract capital': ibid 1.4.

[4] Ibid 1.3–1.4.

[5] Ibid 1.8.

This chapter closely examines and scrutinises the ESI program. It discusses the legislative provisions in Subdivision 360-A in detail, and considers a number of proposed technical amendments to these provisions contained in Treasury Laws Amendment (2018 Measures No. 2) Bill 2018.[6] The chapter also examines a number of Australian Taxation Office ('ATO') discussion papers and draft guidelines that deal with various aspects of the ESI program.[7] These documents were issued as part of the ATO's consultation process with stakeholders on the operation of the ESI program.[8] Although the views expressed in these documents are merely preliminary in nature and are not binding on the Commissioner of Taxation, they raise some interesting points on difficult issues that are worthy of further examination.

4.2 Early Stage Innovation Companies

The concept of an ESIC lies at the heart of the ESI program and is an appropriate starting point for examining its operation. Section 360-40 of the ITAA 1997 sets out a number of requirements that a company must satisfy in order to qualify as an ESIC. These requirements may be conveniently divided into two broad categories:

- 'early stage requirements' (see 4.2.1); and
- 'innovation requirements' (see 4.2.2).

4.2.1 Early Stage Requirements

In order for a company to satisfy the early stage requirements in an income year (the 'current year'), it must meet four criteria contained in s 360-40(1). These criteria are tested at 'a particular time', known as the 'test time', which is the time immediately after the company issues the investor with equity interests that are shares in the company.[9] The criteria are as follows:

---

[6] This Bill was introduced into Parliament in February 2018, but had not been passed by the Senate at the time of writing (December 2018).

[7] These documents can be accessed at Australian Taxation Office, *Let's Talk: Tax Incentives for Early Stage Investors* <https://lets-talk.ato.gov.au/ESIC>.

[8] The consultation process opened on 31 October 2017 and closed on 22 January 2018. A final report had not been published at the time of writing.

[9] ITAA 1997 ss 360-15(1)(b), (c), 360-40(1). See also *ESI Explanatory Memorandum* (n 2), which states: 'The time for testing whether an entity is a qualifying ESIC is the time immediately after the relevant equity interests are issued.' The requirement that the investor must be issued equity interests that are shares means that investors who are issued 'debt interests' that are shares (e.g., certain redeemable preference shares) are not eligible for the tax incentive: at 1.29. The distinction between debt and equity interests is determined in accordance with complex tests located in Division 974 of the ITAA 1997: see further R Woellner, S Barkoczy, S Murphy, C Evans and D Pinto, *Australian Taxation Law* (Oxford University Press, 28th ed, 2018) 1135–46.

- **Incorporation criterion.** The company must have been:
  - incorporated in Australia within the last three income years (the latest being the current year);
  - incorporated in Australia within the last six income years (the latest being the current year), and across the last three of those income years it and its 100% subsidiaries[10] (if any) must have incurred total expenses of $1 million or less; or
  - registered in the Australia Business Register within the last three income years (the latest being the current year).[11]
- **Expenses criterion.** The company and its 100% subsidiaries (if any) must have incurred total expenses of $1 million or less in the income year before the current year.[12]
- **Assessable income criterion.** The company and its 100% subsidiaries (if any) must have had total assessable income of $200,000 or less in the income year before the current year.[13]
- **Unlisted criterion.** The company's shares must not be listed for quotation on the official list of any stock exchange in Australia or a foreign country.[14]

Treasury Laws Amendment (2018 Measures No. 2) Bill 2018 proposes to add a fifth criterion to the early stage requirements, which is that the company must not be a 'foreign company' within the meaning of the *Corporations Act 2001* (Cth) ('*Corporations Act*') at the test time.[15]

---

[10] The term '100% subsidiary' is defined in s 975-505 of the ITAA 1997. Basically, a company (the subsidiary company) is a 100% subsidiary of another company (the holding company) if all the shares in the subsidiary company are beneficially owned by: (a) the holding company; (b) one or more 100% subsidiaries of the holding company; or (c) the holding company and one or more 100% subsidiaries of the holding company: s 975-505(1). However, the subsidiary company is not a 100% subsidiary of the holding company if a person is in a position (or will at some future time be in a position) to affect rights, in relation to the subsidiary company, of either the holding company or a 100% subsidiary of the holding company: s 975-505(2), (3).

[11] ITAA 1997 s 360-40(1)(a).

[12] ITAA 1997 s 360-40(1)(b).

[13] ITAA 1997 s 360-40(1)(c). In calculating a company's assessable income, the value of an Accelerating Commercialisation grant under the Entrepreneurs' Programme (discussed below) is expressly disregarded: s 360-40(2).

[14] ITAA 1997 s 360-40(1)(d).

[15] Treasury Laws Amendment (2018 Measures No. 2) Bill 2018 cl 13 of Schedule 2 of Part 2 (proposed s 360-40(1)(f)). The *Corporations Act* defines a foreign company as: (a) a body corporate that is incorporated in an external Territory, or outside Australia and the external Territories, and is not: (i) a corporation sole; or (ii) an exempt public authority; or (b) an unincorporated body that: (i) is formed in an external Territory or outside Australia and the external Territories; and (ii) under the law of its place of formation, may sue or be sued, or may hold property in the name of its secretary or of an officer of the body duly appointed for that purpose; and (iii) does not have its head office or principal place of business in Australia: *Corporations Act* s 9.

Broadly speaking, the early stage requirements are designed to ensure that the ESI program is directed at investments in young, unlisted companies with low expenses and assessable income. Although the criteria appear to be relatively straightforward, some of the provisions are awkwardly drafted and have raised some technical interpretation issues.[16]

One of these issues relates to when a company must be a 100% subsidiary for its income and expenses to be accounted for under the early stage requirements. For example, the question arises as to whether the expenses and assessable income criteria outlined above take into account expenses incurred, or assessable income derived, by entities that were 100% subsidiaries in the previous income year, but are no longer 100% subsidiaries at the test time. The ATO's preliminary view on this question is that the wording of the relevant provisions allows for this.[17] While this view is likely to be correct, it is fair to say that the legislature could have used language that expressed the position more clearly.

Another issue that has arisen concerns the meaning of the phrase 'incurred total expenses'. The ATO's preliminary position on this phrase is that the term 'expenses' refers to amounts which are expenses under general accounting concepts[18] and the

[16] The awkward drafting may have arisen as a result of the fact that the tight implementation timeframe for introducing the ESI program 'put pressure on the level of consultation that was undertaken': Auditor-General, 'Design and Monitoring of the National Innovation and Science Agenda' (Performance Audit No. 10, Australian National Audit Office, 2017) 37.

[17] Australian Taxation Office, 'Issue: When Must a Company be a 100% Subsidiary for its Income and Expenses to be Accounted for Under the ESIC "Early Stage" Tests?' (Discussion Paper, 2017). The ATO explains that 'the view under development is that expense and income amounts are taken into account for each company that was a 100% subsidiary of the potential ESIC, for the period that it was a 100% subsidiary during the relevant test period … This applies whether or not the company is a 100% subsidiary of the potential ESIC at the test time, or for a continuous period before that time': at 1. It should be noted that the ATO acknowledges that there is also an alternate interpretation that 'the expenses and income of a 100% subsidiary are only taken into account if the company was a 100% subsidiary of the ESIC at the test time'. However, it states that this is not its preferred view: at 5.

[18] Australian Taxation Office, 'Issue: Meaning of the Phrase "Incurred Total Expenses" in the Early Stage Innovation Company Tests' (Discussion Paper, 2017) 1. The *ESI Explanatory Memorandum* states that 'total expenses' corresponds to the amount reported by the entity in its previous year's company tax return: *ESI Explanatory Memorandum* (n 2) 1.64, 1.89. However, the ATO explains that the expenses that are reported in the company tax return are the amounts taken from its financial statements: Australian Taxation Office, 'Issue: Meaning of the Phrase "Incurred Total Expenses" in the Early Stage Innovation Company Tests' (n 18) 3. In this regard, the ATO refers to the Australian Accounting Standards Board, which defines 'expenses' as 'decreases in economic benefits during the accounting period in the form of outflows or depletions of assets or incurrences of liabilities that result in decreases in equity, other than those relating to distributions to equity participants': Australian Accounting Standards Board, 'Framework for the Preparation and Presentation of Financial Statements' (Framework, 2004) 27. On this basis, the ATO is of the view that an amount will be an expense where 'it results in a decrease in the equity of the potential ESIC, otherwise than by way of a distribution to its members': Australian Taxation Office, 'Issue: Meaning of the Phrase "Incurred Total Expenses" in the Early Stage Innovation Company Tests' (n 18) 3. One consequence of this interpretation is that an outgoing which has been properly capitalised, and which results in the recognition of an asset under ordinary accounting concepts will

term 'incurred' has the same jurisprudential meaning as it does in s 8-1 of the ITAA 1997.[19] The use of a 'hybrid approach', which combines accounting and jurisprudential concepts to interpret the phrase, has been criticised by one commentator who argues that this was 'not the legislative intent' and that the approach is 'practically difficult and unworkable'.[20]

Finally, there is also an issue relating to the operation of the 'three year expense test' in the second limb of the incorporation criterion. The issue is whether expenses incurred after the test time but which are nevertheless still incurred in the 'current year' should be included in calculating the total expenses for the purposes of the $1 million threshold. The ATO's preliminary view is that only those expenses that have been incurred at the test time should be included.[21] To resolve this issue, the Government is proposing to amend the provision by inserting the words 'before the current year' after the words 'those income years'.[22] This change is designed to ensure that companies will know at the test time whether this criterion is satisfied.[23]

---

not be taken into account as an expense as any outgoing of cash or increase in liabilities is offset by the recognition of a new asset. Accordingly, the ATO rejects the view that the word expense should take its plain ordinary meaning of money paid or spent: at 4.

[19] Australian Taxation Office, 'Issue: Meaning of the Phrase "Incurred Total Expenses" in the Early Stage Innovation Company Tests' (n 18) 1. The cases dealing with s 8-1 (as well as its predecessor, s 51(1) of the *Income Tax Assessment Act 1936* (Cth)) have indicated that a 'presently existing liability' must have arisen for an outgoing to be incurred: see *Nilsen Development Laboratories Pty Ltd v FC of T* 81 ATC 4031, 4037 (per Barwick CJ); *Coles Myer Finance Ltd v FC of T* 93 ATC 4214, 4222 (per Mason CJ, Brennan, Dawson, Toohey and Gaudron JJ).

[20] Dragan Misic, 'New Approach to Capital Raising: Tax Perspective' (2017) 21(2) *The Tax Specialist* 65, 66. Misic argues that the problem with the hybrid approach is that it requires 'one to test whether an expense is an expense for accounting purposes, then to notionally test whether such an expense was "incurred" taking into account the extensive jurisprudence on this term.'

[21] Australian Taxation Office, 'Issue: 3-Year Expense Test and Expenditure Incurred After the Test Time in Tax Incentives for Early Stage Company Investors' (Discussion Paper, 2017) 1. This view is based on the use of the phrase 'at a particular time' which appears in s 360-40(1) (and also s 360-15(1) (see 4.3)) and which indicates that the test is to be applied at a specific point in time within the relevant year. The ATO points out that its interpretation: is consistent with the objective of determining whether the company is at an early stage of its development at the time of investment; promotes certainty, by enabling a potential investor to determine their eligibility for the offset; and ensures that an investor does not become retrospectively ineligible as a result of the company's expenditure of the invested funds: at 3.

[22] Treasury Laws Amendment (2018 Measures No. 2) Bill 2018 cl 12 of Schedule 2 of Part 2.

[23] Explanatory Memorandum, Treasury Laws Amendment (2018 Measures No. 2) Bill 2018 (Cth), 2.52.

4.2.2 *Innovation Requirements*

The innovation requirements are more controversial than the early stage requirements and are likely to be more problematic in practice. There are two alternative tests that can be used to determine whether a company meets the innovation requirements:

- the '100 point test' (also referred to as the 'gateway test'); and
- the 'principles-based test' (also referred to as the 'alternative test').[24]

Each of these tests has their own complex criteria, which are discussed below.[25]

4.2.2.1 100 Point Test

A company will satisfy the 100 point test if it has at least 100 points under s 360-45 of the ITAA 1997 at the test time. Section 360-45(1) contains a table which provides a company with points in eight different circumstances. In addition, s 360-45(2) provides that a company can also receive points for meeting innovation criteria prescribed by regulations.[26]

As the highest number of points awarded under the table is 75 and the lowest is 25, a company will need to meet at least two of the innovation criteria to qualify under the test. It is interesting to note that the highest number of points is awarded if a company satisfies certain criteria relating to the 'R&D tax incentive' and the 'Entrepreneurs' Programme'. Both the R&D tax incentive and the Entrepreneurs' Programme are integral parts of the Government's broader suite of innovation incentive programs, and it is useful to outline how they work before proceeding any further.

---

[24] ITAA 1997 s 360-40(1)(e).

[25] The ATO makes the point that both the early stage test and the innovation requirements must be satisfied by the relevant company issuing the shares (i.e., the 'potential ESIC'). Although the early stage requirements also refer to a potential ESIC's '100% subsidiaries' (see 4.2.1), just because a 100% subsidiary might meet the innovation requirements does not necessarily mean that the potential ESIC will also meet those requirements: Australian Taxation Office, 'Issue: Do the Early Stage Innovation Tests Need to be Satisfied by the Company that Issues Shares to Investors?' (Discussion Paper, 2017).

[26] No regulations have been prescribed for this purpose so far.

The R&D tax incentive provides certain companies, known as 'R&D entities',[27] with tax offsets for expenditure they incur in undertaking 'R&D activities'[28] during an income year.[29] Although the R&D tax incentive is not limited to start-ups and is also available to other companies, companies that have an 'aggregated turnover'[30] of less than $20 million in an income year (which would include start-ups) are entitled to a more generous tax offset than companies that have an aggregated turnover that exceeds this threshold. Generally speaking, companies under the $20 million threshold currently receive a refundable tax offset at the rate of 43.5% of their notional deductions for an income year, while companies above this threshold receive a non-refundable tax offset at the rate of 38.5% of their notional deductions for an income year.[31] An R&D entity's notional deductions for an income

---

[27] An R&D entity is one of the following: (a) a corporation incorporated under an Australian law; (b) a corporation incorporated under a foreign law that is an Australian resident; or (c) a corporation incorporated under a foreign law that is a resident in a country with which Australia has a double tax agreement and which carries on R&D activities through a permanent establishment in Australia: ITAA 1997 s 355-35.

[28] R&D activities consist of 'core R&D activities' and 'supporting R&D activities': ITAA 1997 s 355-20. Core R&D activities are defined as experimental activities:

(a) whose outcome cannot be known or determined in advance on the basis of current knowledge, information or experience, but can only be determined by applying a systematic progression of work that:
   (i) is based on principles of established science; and
   (ii) proceeds from hypothesis to experiment, observation and evaluation, and leads to logical conclusions; and
(b) that are conducted for the purpose of generating new knowledge (including new knowledge in the form of improved materials, products, devices, processes or services): s 355-25(1).

Certain activities are expressly deemed not to be core R&D activities: s 355-25(2). Supporting R&D activities are activities 'directly related' to core R&D activities: s 355-30. However, activities covered by the exclusions in s 355-25(2) or that produce, or are directly related to producing, goods or services are supporting R&D activities only if they are undertaken for the dominant purpose of supporting core R&D activities.

[29] ITAA 1997 s 355-100. An R&D entity is only entitled to claim the tax offset if it has been registered by ISA for its R&D activities for the relevant income year. The registration process take place under Div 2 of Pt III of the *Industry Research and Development Act 1986* (Cth). Companies have 10 months from the end of their income year to lodge an application for registration of the R&D activities they conducted in the previous year.

[30] The term aggregated turnover is defined in s 328-120 of the ITAA 1997.

[31] ITAA 1997 s 355-100(1). Special rules apply if an R&D entity's notional deductions are under $20,000 for an income year: s 355-100(2). Where an R&D entity's notional deductions for an income year exceed $100 m, it is entitled to a tax offset of only 30% on the excess amount: s 355-100(3). It is important to note that the Government is proposing to make significant changes to the operation of the R&D tax incentive, including changing the way that the rates of tax offset are

year are calculated by reference to its 'R&D expenditure'[32] for the year as well as certain other amounts.[33]

The Entrepreneur's Programme provides qualifying businesses with various kinds of support, including grants, advice from industry experts and facilitated opportunities for collaboration.[34] Like the R&D tax incentive, this support is available to a range of entities and not just to start-ups. Nevertheless, one element of the program that start-ups can particularly benefit from is the Accelerating Commercialisation grant.[35] This grant is targeted at assisting entrepreneurs to commercialise a novel product, process or service. The grant can be up to $1 million and provides up to 50% of the eligible expenditure incurred in relation to a commercialisation project.[36]

Linking the 100 point test to the R&D tax incentive and the Entrepreneurs' Programme has clearly been a strategic decision by the Government and demonstrates that it is taking a multi-pronged approach to supporting start-ups. It recognises that companies that qualify for support under these other programs would have already met various innovation-related criteria that would suggest they are also worthy of being supported under the ESI program.

Table 4.1 sets out the 100 point test. The first three columns of the table are as they appear in s 360-45(1). The fourth column contains our additional commentary on each criterion.

---

calculated: see Treasury Laws Amendment (Making Sure Multinationals Pay Their Fair Share of Tax in Australia and Other Measures) Bill 2018 (Cth).

[32] ITAA 1997 s 355-205. Broadly speaking, R&D expenditure is expenditure incurred on one or more R&D activities (see n 28) for which the R&D entity is registered under s 27A of the *Industry Research and Development Act 1986* for the relevant income year and that fall within the kinds of R&D activities listed in s 355-210.

[33] These amounts are contained in ITAA 1997 ss 355-305, 355-315, 355-480, 355-520, 355-525, 355-580.

[34] See further Australian Government, *Entrepreneurs' Programme*, Business.gov.au, <https://www.business.gov.au/assistance/entrepreneurs-programme-summary>.

[35] Accelerating Commercialisation grants are available to entities with less than $20 million annual turnover for each of the last three financial years, and are assessed on a competitive basis according to how well the entity meets the relevant merit criteria: Department of Industry, Innovation and Science, 'Entrepreneurs' Programme – Programme Guidelines Version 10' (Programme Guidelines, December 2018) cls 123, 125–8, 141, 144–6.

[36] Ibid cl 118. A commercialisation project must aim to achieve at least one of the following: complete the development of a novel product, process or service; prove the commercial viability of a novel product, process or service; make the first sales of a novel product, process or service; or guide the applicant towards the commercialisation of its novel product, process or service: at cl 133.

Table 4.1 The 100 point test and additional commentary

Item	Points	Innovation criteria	Commentary
1	75	At least 50% of the company's total expenses for the previous income year is expenditure that the company can notionally deduct for that income year under section 355-205 (about R&D expenditure).	Strictly speaking, R&D is not by itself innovation, since it occurs before a new idea is actually implemented and commercialised. The Government nevertheless recognises that there are important links between R&D and innovation and it has noted that where a company spends a 'significant amount' on R&D, this is likely to be a strong indicator that it is focused on commercialisation.[a] On this basis, this item awards a significant number of points to those companies that can notionally deduct at least half of their expenditure for an income year as R&D expenditure.
2	75	The company has received an Accelerating Commercialisation Grant under the program administered by the Commonwealth known as the Entrepreneurs' Programme.	The Accelerating Commercialisation grant assists companies with their commercialisation projects. The Government considers that a company that has received an Accelerating Commercialisation grant is 'likely to also meet the principle-based definition of a qualifying ESIC'.[b] This is presumably because the eligibility criteria for such a grant also contain a number of related innovation and commercialisation requirements.
3	50	At least 15%, but less than 50%, of the company's total expenses for the previous income year is expenditure that the company can notionally deduct for that income year under section 355-205 (about R&D expenditure).	This item is an alternative to item 1. The lower number of points available under this item reflects the fact that a lesser proportion of the company's expenditure is R&D expenditure.

4	50	(a) the company has completed or is undertaking an accelerator program that: (i) provides time-limited support for entrepreneurs with start-up businesses; and (ii) is provided to entrepreneurs that are selected in an open, independent and competitive manner; and (b) the entity providing that program has been providing that, or other accelerator programs for entrepreneurs, for at least 6 months; and (c) such programs have been completed by at least one cohort of entrepreneurs.	The legislation does not define an accelerator program. Generally speaking, accelerator programs are run by organisations that provide groups of start-ups with a range of services (such as working space, training and mentoring) to help accelerate their growth.[c] These programs may be run for-profit or not for-profit. Draft guidelines published by the ATO have identified the following five key features of accelerators:[d] (1) accelerators typically provide start-ups with seed funding in exchange for a small amount of equity;[e] (2) accelerators simultaneously invest in a cohort of start-ups;[f] (3) accelerators often require start-ups to be co-located full-time in the same space;[g] (4) accelerators deliver structured programs that are of a fixed term and limited duration;[h] and (5) accelerators provide mentoring support.[i] The draft guidelines, however, go on to state that an eligible accelerator program need not necessarily meet all these characteristics, and that eligibility will be considered on a case-by-case basis. To be an eligible accelerator program, it is critical that the support is available for only a limited time[j] and that entrepreneurs are selected through a merit-based screening process.[k] In addition, to minimise manipulation opportunities, the provider must have provided the program, or other accelerator programs, for at least 6 months and at least one cohort of entrepreneurs must have completed such programs.[l]

(continued)

Table 4.1 (continued)

Item	Points	Innovation criteria	Commentary
5	50	(a) a total of at least $50,000 has been paid for equity interests that are shares in the company; and (b) the company issued those shares to one or more entities that: (i) were not associates of the company immediately before the issue of those shares; and (ii) did not acquire those shares primarily to assist another entity become entitled to a tax offset (or a modified CGT treatment) under this Subdivision; and (c) the company issued those shares at least one day before the test time.	This item applies where an unassociated third party (such as an angel) has invested a significant amount of capital in an investee company at least one day before the shares are issued. An investment of this kind signals a degree of confidence in the company's future prospects from an independent investor. Importantly, the third party must not be an associate of the company immediately before the shares are issued. The term 'associate' is defined widely in the legislation.[m] The definition covers the following entities: • a partner of the company or a partnership in which the company is a partner; • a trustee of a trust estate under which the company or its associate benefits; • another entity that, acting alone or with another entity or entities, sufficiently influences the company; • an entity that, either alone or together with associates, holds a majority voting interest in the company; • a second company that is sufficiently influenced by the company or the company's associates; and • a second company in which a majority voting interest is held by the company or the company's associates.[n]
6	50	(a) the company has rights (including equitable rights) under a Commonwealth law as: (i) the patentee, or a licensee, of a standard patent; or (ii) the owner, or a licensee, of a plant breeder's right; granted in Australia within the last 5 years (ending at the test time); or (b) the company has equivalent rights under a foreign law.	The Government considers that a company that holds a standard patent or plant breeder's right is likely to be focused on the commercialisation of a new or significantly improved product, process, service, marketing or organisational method. Furthermore, the company is likely to have already gone through a 'rigorous registration process' in securing its rights.[o] In Australia, a standard patent is examined by IP Australia before it is granted and protects an invention for up to 20 years.[p] The invention claimed in a standard patent must be 'new, involve an inventive step and be able to be made or used in an industry'.[q] Plant breeder's rights are 'exclusive commercial rights' for a registered variety of plant.[r] Eligible new or recently exploited varieties of plants can be registered, and protection applies for 20 years for most plant species, and 25 years for vines and trees.[s]

7	25	Unless item 6 applies to the company at the test time: (a) the company has rights (including equitable rights) under a Commonwealth law as: (i) the patentee, or a licensee, of an innovation patent granted and certified in Australia; or (ii) the owner, or a licensee, of a registered design registered in Australia; within the last 5 years (ending at the test time); or (b) the company has equivalent rights under a foreign law.	The Government considers that a company that holds an innovation patent or registered design is also likely to be focused on commercialisation and will have gone through a rigorous registration process in securing the rights.[t] This item is mutually exclusive to item 6, meaning that if a company has already received points under item 6, it cannot also receive points under this item. This item is worth fewer points than item 6 because an innovation patent is less valuable than a standard patent. Whereas a standard patent provides long-term protection and control over an invention, an innovation patent only lasts up to eight years,[u] and is designed to protect inventions that do not demonstrate the 'inventive step' required for a standard patent.[v] An innovation patent represents a much quicker and easier way to obtain protection than a standard patent. Unlike a standard patent, an innovation patent is not examined by IP Australia prior to being granted. This means that an innovation patent will only be legally enforceable if it is examined.[w] The term design, in relation to a product, refers to the overall appearance of the product resulting from one or more of its 'visual features' (i.e., the shape, configuration, pattern or ornamentation of the product).[x] As with innovation patents, registered designs are also not automatically legally enforceable. While registration protects a design for five years, it is only once the design has been examined and certified by the Registrar of Designs that it becomes legally enforceable.[y]
8	25	The company has a written agreement with: (a) an institution or body listed in Schedule 1 to the *Higher Education Funding Act 1988* (about institutions or bodies eligible for special research assistance); or (b) an entity registered under section 29A of the *Industry Research and Development Act 1986* (about research service providers); to co-develop and commercialise a new, or significantly improved, product, process, service or marketing or organisational method.	The Government recognises that start-ups will not always have the resources to undertake their commercialisation projects alone. With this in mind, it is accepted that start-ups that have an agreement to work with the organisations set out under this item are likely to be commercialising worthwhile innovations. To qualify, the agreement must provide that the start-up and the relevant organisation will co-develop and commercialise a new, or significantly improved, product, process, service or marketing or organisational method. Institutions listed in Schedule 1 to the *Higher Education Funding Act 1988* are all specified universities or other tertiary education institutions. Entities registered under section 29A of the *Industry Research and Development Act 1986* are known as 'research service providers', and are organisations that have been registered by the Department of Industry, Innovation and Science (on behalf of ISA). They can provide scientific or technical expertise, and have resources to perform R&D on behalf of other companies.[z]

(continued)

Table 4.1 (continued)

[a]*ESI Explanatory Memorandum* (n 2) 1.91.
[b]Ibid 1.94
[c]See further, Australian Taxation Office, *Qualifying as an Early Stage Innovation Company* (2 August 2017) <https://www.ato.gov.au/Business/Tax-incentives-for-innovation/In-detail/Tax-incentives-for-early-stage-investors/?page=2#100_point_innovation_test_requirements>.
[d]Australian Taxation Office, 'Eligibility of Accelerator Programs under the 100-Point Innovation Test' (2017); see also UNSW Australia Business School, 'The Role and Performance of Accelerators in the Australian Startup Ecosystem' (Final Report for the Department of Industry, Innovation and Science, 2016).
[e]The amount of equity is generally around 7.5% to 10% for a $20,000 to $50,000 cash investment: Australian Taxation Office, 'Eligibility of Accelerator Programs under the 100-Point Innovation Test' (n d).
[f]Entry is usually limited to up to 10 start-ups per cohort: ibid.
[g]The reason for this is that the sharing of resources provides economies of scale and facilitates peer interaction: ibid.
[h]The programs are typically three to six months long and often highly intensive: ibid.
[i]This support can come from program alumni, business advisors, entrepreneurs, angels and/or venture capitalists: ibid.
[j]The short three to six months time-frame together with the intense level of support provided to the relevant start-ups differentiates accelerators from 'incubators'. Incubators tend to house start-ups for much longer periods of around one to five years and often do not have clear graduation dates for their companies.
[k]The merit-based screening process is necessary because of the requirement that entrepreneurs must be selected in an open, independent and competitive manner. Programs that allow entry predominantly based on a fee are therefore unlikely to be eligible. The Government has noted that companies that have been selected through a merit-based screening process are also likely to meet the principles-based test: *ESI Explanatory Memorandum* (n 2) 1.96.
[l]Australian Taxation Office, 'Eligibility of Accelerator Programs under the 100-Point Innovation Test' (n l).
[m]*Income Tax Assessment Act 1936* (Cth) s 318.
[n]Australian Tax Office, *Qualifying as an Early Stage Innovation Company* (n c).
[o]*ESI Explanatory Memorandum* (n 2) 1.103.
[p]*Patents Act 1990* (Cth) ss 43A-45, 67; IP Australia, *Types of Patents* (30 May 2016) <https://www.ipaustralia.gov.au/patents/understanding-patents/types-patents#standard>. The grant of a patent can take from six months up to several years and can be a costly process.

[q]IP Australia, *Types of Patents* (n p); *Patents Act 1990* (Cth) s 18. The *Patents Act 1990* (Cth) defines an inventive step in the following way: 'an invention is to be taken to involve an inventive step when compared with the prior art base unless the invention would have been obvious to a person skilled in the relevant art in the light of the common general knowledge as it existed (whether in or out of the patent area) before the priority date of the relevant claim': s 7.

[r]Plant breeder's rights encourage plant breeding and innovation, whilst ensuring that 'a large and growing pool of new plant varieties is freely available to anybody when the protection periods lapse': IP Australia, *PBR Basics* (19 April 2018) <https://www.ipaustralia.gov.au/plant-breeders-rights/understanding-pbr>.

[s]*Plant Breeder's Rights Act 1994* (Cth) ss 22, 43.

[t]*ESI Explanatory Memorandum* (n 2) 1.103.

[u]*Patents Act 1990* (Cth) s 68.

[v]Note that the Government is currently considering phasing out innovation patents, which could impact this item: IP Australia, *Phasing Out of the Innovation Patent System* <https://www.ipaustralia.gov.au/policy-register/phasing-out-of-the-innovation-patent-system>.

[w]IP Australia, *Types of Patents* (n p).

[x]*Design Act 2003* (Cth) ss 5, 7, 67.

[y]IP Australia, *Registration and Certification* (3 March 2016) <https://www.ipaustralia.gov.au/designs/understanding-designs/registration-and-certification>; *Design Act 2003* (Cth) ss 5, 46.

[z]Business.gov.au, *Research Service Providers: Using a Research Service Provider (RSP) to Conduct R&D* (5 April 2018) <https://www.business.gov.au/assistance/research-and-development-tax-incentive/research-service-providers>.

Example
Alpha Co is a start-up company that meets the ESI program's early stage requirements. Alpha Co is developing a new lightweight synthetic material for use in manufacturing high-performance running shoes for athletes. It received a previous investment of $60,000 from an angel investor who is unaffiliated with the company (50 points). It also recently received an Accelerating Commercialisation grant under the Entrepreneurs' Programme (75 points). As Alpha Co has 125 points, it satisfies the 100 point test. It therefore qualifies as an ESIC and does not need to consider the principles-based test.

4.2.2.2 Principles-Based Test

A company satisfies the principles-based test if it meets the following five criteria at the test time:

- **Commercialisation criterion.**[37] The company is genuinely focused on developing for commercialisation one or more new, or significantly improved, products, processes, services or marketing or organisational methods.
- **High growth criterion.** The business relating to those products, processes, services or methods has a high growth potential.
- **Scalability criterion.** The company can demonstrate that it has the potential to successfully scale that business.
- **Wide market criterion.** The company can demonstrate that it has the potential to address a broader than local market, including global markets, through that business.
- **Competitive advantage criterion.** The company can demonstrate that it has the potential to be able to have competitive advantages for that business.[38]

As the above criteria are cumulative, a company that fails to meet even one criterion will not satisfy the principles-based test. The ATO's draft guidelines indicate that in order to demonstrate that it satisfies the principles-based test, a company must be able to show that 'tangible steps have been or will be taken' in relation to each of the criteria.[39] It can use existing documentation to demonstrate this, including business plans, commercialisation strategies or competition analyses.[40]

---

[37] The commercialisation criterion highlights 'the distinction between simply having an idea and generating economic value from that idea': *ESI Explanatory Memorandum* (n 2) 1.81. The language used in this criterion is consistent with the definition of innovation contained in the OECD's Oslo Manual: see OECD, *OSLO Manual: Guidelines for Collecting and Interpreting Innovation Data* (OECD, 3rd ed, 2005) 46.

[38] ITAA 1997 s 360-40.

[39] Australian Taxation Office, 'A Step-by-Step Guide to the Principles-Based Innovation Test' (2017) 20.

[40] Ibid.

A special exclusion provides that the principles-based test cannot be satisfied in relation to a product, process, service or method, or an improvement to a product, process, service or method, of a kind that is prescribed in the regulations.[41] Likewise, a company does not qualify as an ESIC if, before the test time, it engaged in an activity prescribed by the regulations.[42] So far, no regulations have been made for either of these purposes.[43]

Example

Beta Co is a start-up company that meets the ESI program's early stage requirements. Beta Co is developing an innovative piece of engineering software that will be delivered to users via a mobile app. Beta Co holds a standard patent in relation to its software (50 points under the 100 point test), but does not satisfy any other criteria under the 100 point test. Beta Co must therefore satisfy the principles-based test to qualify as an ESIC.

Beta Co is genuinely focused on developing its innovative software for commercialisation and has no other activities. Its business has high growth potential as once its software has been fully tested, it will be able to be launched over the internet using the app. This will allow Beta Co to tap into a wide market and rapidly grow its revenue. Beta Co's business is scalable because it will be able to deliver its product to a large number of customers over the internet with little increase in operating costs. The company will service a wide market because it anticipates being able to license its software in both Australia and overseas. It also has a competitive advantage over other companies because its software is more user-friendly and faster than software used for similar tasks. Beta Co is therefore likely to satisfy the principles-based test and qualify as an ESIC.

4.2.3 *Critique of the Innovation Requirements*

Both the 100 point test and the principles-based test have been criticised by various commentators. For example, in relation to the 100 point test, it has been suggested that some of the criteria will not yet be relevant to certain start-ups,[44] and that several criteria 'require material expenditure which many early stage companies will be

[41] ITAA 1997 s 360-40(3).

[42] ITAA 1997 s 360-40(4).

[43] The Government has emphasised that it is important to ensure that any exclusions should not extend to 'truly innovative products, services and activities': Australian Government, 'Tax Incentives for Early Stage Investors' (Policy Discussion Paper, 2016) 5.

[44] Michael Phillips, *Tax Incentives for Investors in Early Stage Investment Companies* (18 May 2016) Swaab <http://www.swaab.com.au/Publications/Publications/Tax-Incentives-for-Investors-in-Early-Stage-Invest?utm_source=Mondaq&utm_medium=syndication&utm_campaign=View-Original>.

unable to fund.'[45] It is acknowledged that there will certainly be some start-ups that are at such an early stage of development that they will not yet be in a position to qualify for points under the 100 point test. Likewise, there will also be some start-ups that may only be able to satisfy one of the eight categories and will therefore not have enough points to qualify. Notwithstanding this, although one commentator has described the 100 point test as 'potentially vague and complex',[46] we consider that, on the whole, it provides objective criteria that should be relatively straightforward to apply and is therefore an appropriate gateway test. It does, however, need to be acknowledged that the test will only be able to be met by certain start-ups,[47] and, for this reason, it is anticipated that a significant number of companies seeking ESIC status are likely to do so on the basis of the more flexible principles-based test. The problem with this test, however, is that it is based on a range of abstract criteria that can be difficult to apply.[48]

Under the principles-based test, even basic concepts, such as determining whether a product, process, service or marketing or organisational method (hereinafter referred to as an 'innovation') is 'new' or 'significantly improved', will not necessarily be straightforward.[49] The Explanatory Memorandum states that for an innovation to meet this criterion, it must be new or significantly improved for the

---

[45] Carlos Gouveia, *Early Stage Innovation Companies – 10 Months On* (27 April 2017) Colin Biggers & Paisley Lawyers <https://www.cbp.com.au/insights/2017/april/early-stage-innovation-companies-10-months-on>.

[46] Phillips (n 44).

[47] Bailey is nevertheless of the view that 'most quality start-ups should be able to qualify using the 100 point test': Michael Bailey, 'Early Stage Innovation Company Investor Tax Breaks Misunderstood', *Australian Financial Review* (online), 4 May 2017 <http://www.afr.com/leadership/entrepreneur/early-stage-innovation-company-investor-tax-breaks-misunderstood-by-founders-investors-20170504-gvyr4x#ixzz4idVpA5H7>.

[48] It has been noted that: 'Although deliberately broad in its application, the principles-based test is, by no means, easy to self-assess with confidence': Jessica Brass and Mark Trewhella, 'Early Stage Innovation Companies – A Deeper Dive' (2017) 51(8) *Taxation in Australia* 427, 428.

[49] The ATO draft guidelines explain in detail the meaning of innovation in relation to products, processes, services and methods. According to the guidelines, a 'product innovation' constitutes 'the introduction of a good or service that is new or significantly improved with respect to its functional characteristics or intended uses within its addressable market. This includes significant improvements in technical specifications, components and materials, incorporated software, user-friendliness or other functional characteristics': Australian Taxation Office, 'A Step-by-Step Guide to the Principles-Based Innovation Test' (n 39) 6. A 'process innovation' is described as 'the implementation of a new or significantly improved production or delivery method', which may include significant changes in systems, techniques, equipment or software: at 8. Likewise, a 'marketing method' innovation is described as 'the implementation of a new or significantly improved marketing method involved in product design or packaging, product placement, product promotion or pricing aimed at better addressing customer needs, opening up new markets, or re-positioning a company's product within the market, with the objective of increasing sales': at 9. Finally, the guidelines describe an 'organisational method' innovation as 'the implementation of a new or significantly improved organisational method in the company's business practices, workplace organisation or external relations', noting that innovations 'can be aimed at increasing organisational performance by reducing administrative or transaction costs, improving labour productivity, or reducing the cost of supplies': at 10.

'applicable addressable market'.[50] A company's addressable market is not specifically mentioned in the legislation, but is described in the Explanatory Memorandum as 'the available revenue opportunity or market demand arising from the innovation, or the business relating to that innovation'.[51] While the Explanatory Memorandum states that the addressable market must be objectively and realistically identified, it is conceivable that investors and the ATO may, quite legitimately, form different views on what constitutes a company's addressable market. A simple scenario would be where the ATO might argue that a company's addressable market is Australia, whereas an investor might argue that it is merely a particular State or city within the country. In theory, it will be harder to show that an innovation is new or significantly improved if the addressable market is defined widely than if it is defined narrowly. This is because it is less likely that something is new or significantly improved in a large market than a small one. In identifying the addressable market for an innovation, it is necessary to consider a range of matters, including the location and characteristics of potential customers that are likely to use the innovation and the area or industry that is to be serviced by the innovation.[52] While an addressable market could be a completely new market created by the innovation, most innovations are likely to cater for existing markets.

For the purposes of determining whether an innovation is new or significantly improved, it is necessary to closely consider the features of the innovation, including its constituent components, technical design, functional characteristics and user-friendliness. These features need to be compared with what already exists in the marketplace. A product, process, service or method is new where it is novel, and it is significantly improved where it is much better than what came before it.[53] Modifications to a product, process, service or method that result in only minor functional improvements will not be sufficient for it to be regarded as new or significantly improved.[54]

Assuming that a company can show that it has a new or significantly improved product, process, service or marketing or organisation method, it must still demonstrate that it is 'genuinely focused' on 'developing' this innovation for 'commercialisation' in order to satisfy the first criterion. The ATO's draft guidelines provide some interpretive assistance on the meaning of these expressions. The draft guidelines state that the phrase 'genuinely focused' 'looks to the activity on which

[50] *ESI Explanatory Memorandum* (n 2) 1.79.

[51] Ibid.

[52] The ATO draft guidelines set out some other features that may help to identify a company's addressable market. These include the product market, the type of customer or industry to be served and the timing of the supply: Australian Taxation Office, 'A Step-by-Step Guide to the Principles-Based Innovation Test' (n 39) 6.

[53] See also ibid 5.

[54] In this regard, the Explanatory Memorandum warns: 'Improvements resulting from the customisation of existing products, minor extensions such as updates to existing equipment or software, changes to pricing strategies, changes to goods resulting from cyclical or seasonal change and the trading of new products for a wholesaler, retail outlet or distribution business where activities are similar to the approach of competitors are unlikely to satisfy the significantly improved threshold': *ESI Explanatory Memorandum* (n 2) 1.80.

the company is truly concentrating' its attention, and that the company's 'intention and purpose' must be considered (presumably judged by reference to the intention of its directors).[55] The draft guidelines define 'developing' in this context as 'the process of creating an innovation or causing it to change or evolve, to the point where it can be commercialised', while 'commercialisation' is said to refer to 'commercial exploitation of an innovation through the sale, introduction or implementation of that innovation in its addressable market, which directly leads to the generation of economic value for the company'.[56] According to the draft guidelines, it is not sufficient for a company to have an innovation; it must develop the innovation 'sufficiently beyond the pre-concept stage' by 'undertaking activities and taking tangible steps with the intention of commercially exploiting the innovation'.[57]

In a similar vein, while 'high growth potential', 'potential to be able to successfully scale', 'potential to be able to address a broader than local market' and 'potential to be able to have competitive advantages' refer to widely understood concepts in a general sense, they can be inherently difficult to appraise or measure.[58] This stems from the fact that they are based on loose marketing and economic concepts that do not have strict legal definitions. In this regard, one of the main concerns that has been levelled at the principles-based test is that it contains 'highly subjective

[55] Australian Taxation Office, 'A Step-by-Step Guide to the Principles-Based Innovation Test' (n 39) 12. The draft guidelines also set out a number of practical ways that a company can demonstrate its 'genuine focus'.

[56] Ibid 11. Activities that the draft guidelines list as demonstrating 'development' of an innovation include: proof of concept activities, market research, prototyping, pilots and user testing, setting up manufacturing and marking processes and other activities to prepare for the launch of the innovation.

[57] Ibid. Activities that are not contemplated as satisfying the 'developing for commercialisation' requirement by the draft guidelines include experimental R&D activities, activities involving implementation of an innovation to other parts of a business after the initial implementation, and activities in the innovation's addressable market where the company has already made its first sales and is no longer developing the innovation: at 11.

[58] The ATO's draft guidelines describe 'growth potential' as 'a company's ability to generate larger revenue, expand its workforce, increase production and broaden its market in the future', and note that in order to meet this criterion, a company 'must have the potential to significantly increase its economic value through expansion'. Ways that a company may do this include developing new products, broadening its customer base or entering new markets: ibid 13. In relation to 'potential to be able to successfully scale', the draft guidelines note that the company must demonstrate 'that it is or will be capable of scaling up its business' to fill its high growth potential. In order to be able to successfully scale, the company's relevant activity 'must be of a kind that is not prevented from significant growth by elements intrinsic to its nature', and the business must not 'face any inherent restriction from multiplying in its size and scale'. Where a company's activity is scalable 'its existing revenues can be multiplied while incurring a reduced or minimal increase in operating costs': at 13–4. A company's 'potential to be able to address a broader than local market' means, according to the draft guidelines, that the company 'must have the potential to serve a market that is broader than a local city, area or region' and that the company's business must be capable of being adapted to supply a broader market in the future: at 14. Finally, the draft guidelines define a 'competitive advantage' as 'an attribute that allows a company to outperform its competitors (including any new competitors)', generally being either a 'differential advantage' (whereby the company's innovation can deliver benefits to customers greater than those offered by competing products or services) or a 'cost advantage' (whereby the company has a lower cost per unit than its competitors): at 15.

language'.[59] People are likely to bring their own perspectives and individual biases to interpreting the criteria, and this can arguably lead to different conclusions depending on how the words are construed.

It has also been noted that the principles-based test involves a degree of 'crystal ball gazing'.[60] This is due to the fact that it requires a company to demonstrate its 'potential' to do certain things, which inherently involves some form of speculation as to its future capability. It is likely to be the newer companies that will have the greatest difficulty in addressing the criteria as their businesses and innovations may not yet be sufficiently developed for them to be able to make meaningful predictions.

The principles-based test also raises a fundamental interpretation issue, namely whether the relevant criteria should be determined objectively or subjectively. While, as mentioned above, a company's 'genuine focus' on developing an innovation for commercialisation may take the company's subjective intention into account, it is nevertheless submitted that issues such as 'high growth potential', 'potential to be able to successfully scale', 'potential to be able to address a broader than local market' and 'potential to be able to have competitive advantages' should all be determined objectively.

The reality is that although the principles-based test has been expressly designed to provide flexibility to cover 'future innovations',[61] there are likely to be several borderline cases where it will be difficult to ascertain whether the criteria are met. Ultimately, this is anticipated to fuel requests for tax rulings and could potentially result in litigation in contentious cases. In this regard, it has been suggested by one commentator that 'most taxpayers would use this test as a last resort' given the difficulty of demonstrating that it has been met satisfactorily.[62] The challenges associated with applying the principles-based test are perhaps not surprising given that innovation is inherently a 'nebulous' concept; just as it is difficult to predict future innovations, it is also difficult to create a test for identifying them.[63]

4.2.4 Tax Rulings

It is important to recognise that under Australia's self-assessment system of taxation, the risk of incorrectly claiming the ESI tax incentives lies with investors. Investors who incorrectly claim the incentives stand to have their assessments

---

[59] Phillips (n 44).

[60] Brass and Trewhella (n 48) 428.

[61] *ESI Explanatory Memorandum* (n 2) 1.76.

[62] Misic (n 20) 67.

[63] The ATO website provides further information on both innovation tests, as well as a 'decision making tool' that companies can use to help determine their ESIC status: Australian Taxation Office, *Qualifying as an Early Stage Innovation Company* (2 August 2017) <https://www.ato.gov.au/business/tax-incentives-for-innovation/in-detail/tax-incentives-for-early-stage-investors/?page=2#100_point_innovation_test_requirements>; Australian Taxation Office, *ESIC Decision Tool* (22 June 2017) <https://www.ato.gov.au/Calculators-and-tools/ESIC-decision-tool/>.

amended and are exposed to liabilities for interest and penalties.[64] For this reason, it is likely that many investors will not be prepared to invest in a company unless they have some certainty concerning its ESIC status. The principal way that investors can be protected from adverse consequences is under the taxation rulings systems.

Under the taxation rulings system, the Commissioner of Taxation can make both private and public rulings on his interpretation of the income tax laws under Part 5-5 in Schedule 1 of the *Tax Administration Act 1953* ('TAA').[65] A private ruling deals with how a relevant provision applies, or would apply, to a particular entity in relation to a specified scheme.[66] A public ruling, on the other hand, deals with how a relevant provision applies, or would apply, to entities generally, or a class of entities, in relation to a specified scheme or class of schemes.[67] If a ruling applies to an entity and the entity relies on the ruling by acting in accordance with it, the ruling will generally bind the Commissioner.[68] This effectively means that the ATO must apply the law to the entity in the way set out in the ruling and the entity will be protected from having to pay any underpaid tax, penalty or interest in respect of the matters covered by the ruling if it turns out that the ruling is incorrect.

As there are likely to be many situations where uncertainties arise as to whether a company is an ESIC, it is expected that the ATO will receive numerous ruling requests on this issue.[69] Although an investee company can apply for a private ruling as to whether it has satisfied the ESIC tests, a private ruling issued to the company will technically not protect investors given that they are not the actual applicants. While an investor will generally be comforted by seeing a ruling issued to a company stating that it qualifies as an ESIC, the investor is not legally protected under the ruling unless the company applied for the ruling as the investor's agent.[70] Although it is unlikely that the ATO would act contrary to a ruling it has issued to a company, the safest approach would seem to be for investors to apply for rulings

[64] It has been noted that there is no specific 'safe harbour' exception for investors: Mark Gioskos and Travis McCarthy, 'New Tax Incentives for Investors in Start-Up Companies' (2017) 51(7) *Taxation in Australia* 370, 372.

[65] Private rulings are issued under Division 359 and public rulings are issued under Division 358 of Schedule 1 of the TAA.

[66] TAA s 359-5. The ATO's position on private rulings is set out in Australian Taxation Office, *Private Rulings*, TR 2006/11, 4 October 2006 (consolidated ruling 16 August 2017).

[67] TAA s 358-5. The ATO's position on public rulings is set out in Australian Taxation Office, *Public Rulings*, TR 2006/10, 4 October 2006 (consolidated ruling 12 October 2016).

[68] TAA s 357-60.

[69] This has been confirmed in a recent article where it was reported that, as at early May 2017, the ATO had received over 60 private ruling applications since the incentive was introduced on 1 July 2016: Bailey (n 47). The ATO indicated that the vast majority of applicants seeking rulings were using the principles-based test, rather than the 100 point test. This supports the arguments outlined above that the principles-based test is likely to be the more problematic one to apply.

[70] See TAA s 359-10, which states that '[y]ou, your agent or your legal personal representative may apply to the Commissioner for a private ruling'. See also the following comments made by the Commissioner that '[a] ruling applies to you if it is given in response to an application by you' and '[t]he relevant provision must be capable of applying to you personally in order for you to be able to obtain a private ruling on it': Australian Taxation Office, *Private Rulings* (n 66) [20], [29].

themselves.[71] However, as this may cause them extra cost and inconvenience, they may be reluctant to do so in practice.[72]

An alternative approach is that the investee company could apply for a 'class ruling'. Class rulings enable the Commissioner to provide legally binding advice in response to a request 'about the application of a relevant provision to a specific class of entities in relation to a particular scheme'.[73] The purpose of such a ruling 'is to provide certainty to participants and obviate the need for individual participants to seek private rulings.'[74] The practical problem with a class ruling is that as it is a public ruling, it will be available for everyone to see. As many start-ups may not wish to publicly divulge commercially sensitive information about their businesses and innovations, they will generally be reluctant to apply for such rulings.

Whether it is the investor or the company that applies for the ruling, another practical issue that arises is that a company's ESIC status will not be 'protected' by the ruling if the company's circumstances change in the meantime. This is obviously a significant issue for investors, as it can jeopardise their entitlement to the tax offset. The ATO has made it clear that the onus is on investors to 'make enquiries to confirm that there has been no change in the company's activities subsequently to it receiving a ruling that could lead to a different outcome under the tests'.[75]

It is interesting that Parliament did not introduce separate ruling arrangements for the purposes of determining whether a company is an ESIC when it implemented the program. Arguably, because of its special expertise in the innovation arena, ISA may actually be better placed than the ATO to make rulings on this topic. One commentator has stated that ISA may already be providing guidance on these issues in practice, with the decision on ESIC rulings 'typically' being referred to ISA, despite the fact that it is not the decision maker.[76] In this regard, it is worth noting that ISA already plays a key role in the management of the Government's formal venture capital programs, as well as the R&D tax incentive.[77] It is interesting

---

[71] It has been noted that while investors might get some protection if the company provides them with contractual warranties, or even a guarantee or indemnity about their ESIC status, 'this raises the prospect of start-up companies taking on more risk than they otherwise would to attract investors': Gioskos and McCarthy (n 64) 372.

[72] It has also been suggested that there may be cases where investors will find it difficult to apply for private rulings given the information asymmetries that potentially exist between them and their prospective investee companies: Gouveia (n 45).

[73] Australian Taxation Office, *Class Rulings System*, CR 2001/1, 28 February 2001 (consolidated ruling 11 September 2013) [6].

[74] Ibid.

[75] Australian Taxation Office, *For Investors* (2 August 2017) <https://www.ato.gov.au/Business/Tax-incentives-for-innovation/In-detail/Tax-incentives-for-early-stage-investors/?page=4#For_investors>.

[76] Misic (n 20) 67.

[77] ISA dually manages the R&D tax incentive with the ATO. Under this arrangement, the ATO has responsibility for implementing the program, while ISA is empowered to make findings on certain innovation-related matters under the *Industry Research and Development Act 1986* (Cth). These findings are binding on the Commissioner of Taxation.

to observe that at the same time as the ESI program was introduced, ISA was granted a special power to make binding public and private rulings on whether activities are 'not ineligible activities' for the purposes of the VCLP and ESVCLP programs (see 3.4).[78] The Government acknowledged that this change was designed to allow taxpayers to 'obtain certainty about the status of investments for the venture capital tax concessions' from ISA.[79] It is arguable that a similar power should be granted to ISA for the purpose of ruling on whether a company qualifies as an ESIC.

4.3 Tax Offset

From an investor's point of view, one of the main benefits of the ESI program is the availability of a front-end incentive in the form of a tax offset. Section 360-15 provides that an investor is entitled to a tax offset for an income year if:

- the investor is *not* a trust, partnership, widely held company or 100% subsidiary of a widely held company;[80]
- a company issues the investor with equity interests in the form of shares in the company at a particular time during the income year;
- the ESIC requirements in s 360-40 (i.e., the early stage and innovation requirements discussed at Sects. 4.2.1 and 4.2.2) apply to the company immediately after that time;
- neither the investor nor the company are 'affiliates' of each other at that time;[81]
- the issue of the shares is not an acquisition of 'ESS interests' under an employee share scheme;[82] and

---

[78] TAA Division 362. ISA also has the power to make certain determinations in relation to the VCLP and ESVCLP programs under the VC Act, as well as the power to make public and private findings on whether activities within a specified class are 'a substantially novel application of one or more technologies': ITAA 1997 s 118-432. The latter power was granted to ISA in 2018 as a result of the passing of Treasury Laws Amendment (Tax Integrity and Other Measures) Bill 2018 (Cth), Schedule 3, cl 3.

[79] Explanatory Memorandum, Treasury Laws Amendment (Tax Integrity and Other Measures) Bill 2018 (Cth) 3.15.

[80] Treasury Laws Amendment (2018 Measures No. 2) Bill 2018 proposes a change that would have the effect of also specifically excluding ESVCLPs from the list of entities entitled to receive a tax offset: cl 5 of Schedule 2 of Part 2 (proposed s 360-15(1)(ia)). The reasoning behind this proposed exclusion is explained further at 4.3.3.

[81] This requirement ensures that investments are genuine third party investments made for commercial reasons. An 'affiliate' of an entity is an individual or company which acts, or could reasonably be expected to act, in accordance with the entity's directions or wishes, or in concert with the entity. However, an individual or company is not an affiliate merely because of the nature of the business relationship they share with the entity: ITAA 1997 s 328-130.

[82] This requirement ensures that the tax incentive targets new investors who are not connected with the company because of their employment: *ESI Explanatory Memorandum* (n 2) 1.27.

- immediately after that time, the investor does not hold more than 30% of the equity interests in the company or in an entity 'connected'[83] with the company.[84]

As the s 360-40 requirements are tested immediately after the time the shares are issued, an entity's entitlement to the tax offset is not affected if the company subsequently ceases to be an ESIC.[85]

Interestingly, there is no requirement that investors must be Australian residents to claim the tax offset. Foreign residents will, however, only be able to use the tax offset against their Australian tax liability.

4.3.1 Amount of Tax Offset

An entity is generally entitled to a tax offset of 20% of the total amount paid to subscribe for shares in ESICs during an income year.[86] Although the tax offset is not refundable, the amount of any excess tax offset that is not fully utilised in an income year may be carried forward into future income years.[87] Importantly, the tax offset

[83] An entity is 'connected' with another entity if it controls the other entity or is controlled by the other entity, or they are under common control: ITAA 1997 s 328-125.

[84] Treasury Laws Amendment (2018 Measures No. 2) Bill 2018 proposes to change the wording of this requirement. The proposed new wording provides that immediately after the issue of the shares, the investor must not hold 'equity interests in the company, or an entity connected with the company, that carry the right to: (i) receive more than 30% of any distribution of income by the company or the entity; or (ii) receive more than 30% of any distribution of capital by the company or the entity; or (iii) exercise, or control the exercise of, more than 30% of the total voting power in the company or the entity': cl 6 of Schedule 2 of Part 2. The change in wording is designed to ensure that the equity interest test is applied consistently with other parts of the income tax law: Explanatory Memorandum, Treasury Laws Amendment (2018 Measures No. 2) Bill 2018 (Cth) 2.37.

[85] The Explanatory Memorandum notes that: 'a legislative regime that requires ongoing activity checks for a qualifying ESIC ... would impose a regulatory burden on ESICs and create additional risk and uncertainty for investors. That said, it is likely that an entity that has met the requirements to be a qualifying ESIC will remain a qualifying ESIC. To the extent that it stops being a qualifying ESIC, the goal of improving access to capital for that company has been met': *ESI Explanatory Memorandum* (n 2) 1.31–1.32.

[86] ITAA 1997 s 360-25(1). Treasury Laws Amendment (2018 Measures No. 2) Bill 2018 proposes to redraft this section to provide that the amount of the tax offset is 20% of the sum of (a) an amount equal to any money received, or entitled to be received, by the company for the issue of shares; and (b) an amount equal to the market value of any 'non-cash benefit' received, or entitled to be received, by the company for the issue of the shares at the time the shares were issued: cl 8 of Schedule 2 of Part 2. A non-cash benefit can include any property or services that are provided or required to be provided: Explanatory Memorandum, Treasury Laws Amendment (2018 Measures No. 2) Bill 2018 (Cth) 2.42. This clarification is designed to ensure that the services an investor (or a third party) may provide to an investee company are recognised in the calculation of the tax offset.

[87] The tax offset must first be applied against the entity's income tax liability for the relevant income year and any remaining amount may be carried forward into future income years in accordance with the rules contained in Division 65 of the ITAA 1997: s 63-10.

operates subject to a cap, which ensures that an entity (together with its affiliates) cannot claim tax offsets in an income year that exceed $200,000, less any ESI tax offsets that have been carried forward into the income year from a previous year.[88] This means that, subject to special rules for 'retail investors' (see 4.3.2), investors will only be able to claim tax offsets on subscriptions for shares in ESICs up to $1 million in a particular income year. The practical effect of the tax offset is that it will only cost an investor a net amount of $800,000 to acquire $1 million of shares in an ESIC, as the investor will recover $200,000 by way of a tax offset upon lodging their income tax return. The Government is therefore effectively subsidising one-fifth of the investor's investment in the ESIC. This is a generous incentive that should attract considerable interest from angels.

Example
Julie is an experienced angel investor who invests $400,000 in Gamma Co in July 2018, $1,500,000 in Delta Co in September 2018 and $500,000 in Epsilon Co in February 2019. All three companies are ESICs. Julie does not have any carry forward tax offsets.

Julie invested a total of $2,400,000 in ESIC shares in 2018–19, but she is only entitled to a total tax offset of $200,000. If the tax payable on Julie's taxable income for the 2018–19 income year is $170,000, she has an excess non-refundable tax offset of $30,000, which she can carry forward into future income years.

4.3.2 *Restriction on Investments Made by Retail Investors*

A special restriction limits the amount that 'non-sophisticated' or 'non-professional' investors (also generally referred to as 'retail investors') can invest in ESICs. The restriction provides that investors who do not satisfy the 'sophisticated investor'[89] or

---

[88] ITAA 1997 s 360-25(2).

[89] Chapter 6D of the *Corporations Act* requires a company that makes an offer of securities to issue an appropriate 'disclosure document' (such as a prospectus) to investors unless a specific exception (such as the sophisticated and professional investor tests) applies: s 706. The sophisticated investor test is found in sections 708(8) and (10) of the *Corporations Act*. The test will be satisfied under s 708(8) in relation to an offer of securities where: an investor must pay at least $500,000 for the securities; the total amount payable by an investor for the securities, plus any amount paid previously for the company's securities in the same class, is at least $500,000; or an investor has net assets of at least $2.5 million, or gross income for the last two financial years of at least $250,000, as certified by a qualified accountant within 6 months before the offer is made (or the offer is made to a company or trust controlled by a person who meets this requirement). See also Corporations Regulations 2001 (Cth) Reg 6D.2.03. The sophisticated investor test will be satisfied under s 708(10) in relation to an offer of securities where the offer is made to an investor through a financial services licensee, and the licensee is satisfied on reasonable grounds that the investor has previous experience in investing in securities that allows them to make certain assessments, and certain other conditions are fulfilled.

'professional investor'[90] tests found in s 708(8), (10) and (11) of the *Corporations Act* will not be eligible for any tax offset if they invest more than $50,000 in ESIC shares in a financial year.[91] In addition, they will also not receive modified CGT treatment on their shares (see 4.4).[92] The restriction recognises that as investments in ESICs are high risk, retail investors should be protected by being discouraged from making large investments in such companies.[93] The operation of the restriction means that the maximum tax offset that a retail investor will be able to claim each year is limited to $10,000, which is substantially lower than the maximum $200,000 tax offset that sophisticated and professional investors may claim.

Example
Jasmine is a retail investor who invests $10,000 in Delta Co, which is an ESIC, in September 2018. Jasmine is entitled to claim a $2000 tax offset in relation to this investment. In March 2019, Jasmine considers making a $50,000 investment in Epsilon Co, another ESIC. However, because Jasmine does not satisfy the sophisticated or professional investor tests found in ss 708(8), (10), (11) of the *Corporations Act*, she will lose any entitlement to the tax offset if she makes this investment (including entitlement to the tax offset for her investment in Delta Co). Jasmine therefore decides to invest only $40,000 in Epsilon Co. As a result, Jasmine is entitled to claim a total tax offset for the 2018–19 income year of $10,000 ($2000 plus $8000).

---

[90] The professional investor test is found in section 708(11) of the *Corporations Act*. The test will be satisfied in relation to an offer of securities if the offer is made to a 'professional investor' or a person who has or controls gross assets of at least $10 million. Section 9 of the *Corporations Act* defines a professional investor as: a financial services licensee; a body regulated by APRA (the Australian Prudential Regulation Authority) or registered under the *Financial Corporations Act 1974* (Cth); the trustee of a superannuation fund, approved deposit fund, pooled superannuation trust or public sector superannuation scheme (provided the fund, trust or scheme has net assets of at least $10 million); a person who controls at least $10 million; a listed entity or related body corporate of a listed entity; an exempt public authority; a body corporate or unincorporated body that carries on a business of investment in financial products, interests in land or other investments and for those purposes, invests funds received (directly or indirectly) following an offer or invitation to the public, the terms of which provided for the funds subscribed to be invested for those purposes; or a foreign entity that, if established or incorporated in Australia, would be covered by one of the preceding paragraphs.

[91] ITAA 1997 s 360-20.

[92] Australian Taxation Office, *Tax Incentives for Early Stage Investors* (2 August 2017) <https://www.ato.gov.au/Business/Tax-incentives-for-innovation/In-detail/Tax-incentives-for-early-stage-investors/?page=1#The_sophisticated_investor_test>.

[93] The ATO has noted that this limit 'is intended to ensure that the tax incentives don't encourage retail investors to be over-exposed to the risk that is inherent in investing in qualifying ESICs': ibid.

Figure 4.1 sets out a flow-chart for investors trying to work out whether or not the restriction on investments made by retail investors applies to them.

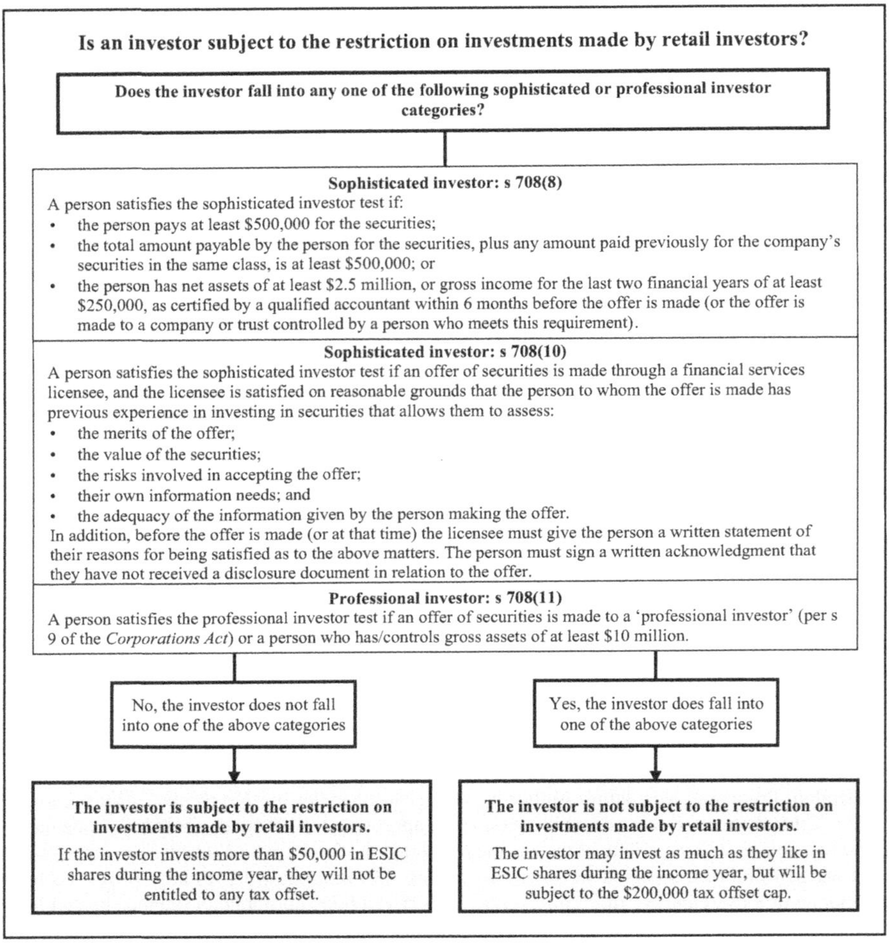

Fig. 4.1 Is the investor subject to the restriction on investments made by retail investors?

4.3.3 *Flow Through of the Tax Offset for Members of Trusts and Partnerships*

Although the tax offset is not available to trusts or partnerships, special rules allow the tax offset to 'flow through' to the members of these entities.[94]Broadly speaking, the beneficiaries of a trust and the partners in a partnership are entitled to their respective shares of the notional tax offset that the trustee or partnership would have otherwise been entitled to receive if it was an individual. This means that the $200,000 annual tax offset cap applies at the trust/partnership level (i.e., the beneficiaries in a trust and partners in a partnership will only receive a share of the tax offset that, in total, does not exceed $200,000).[95] The percentage of the tax offset to which a member is entitled may be determined by the trustee or partnership.[96] However, if the member would be entitled to a fixed portion of any capital gain made by the trust or partnership, the member is entitled to a respective share of the tax offset that is equal to the fixed portion.[97]

The Government is proposing to amend the legislation to ensure that the total ESI tax offset an entity (and its affiliates) can claim in an income year in relation to all direct and indirect investments under the ESI program is limited to $200,000.[98] Currently, the $200,000 limit only applies to direct investments and does not capture situations where entities only make indirect investments through partnerships and trusts. The proposed change will ensure that the $200,000 cap applies 'as a single combined limit'.[99] If implemented, this change would mean that while individuals may be members of multiple trusts and/or partnerships, and may receive a share of an ESI tax offset through more than one of these vehicles, they still could not claim more than $200,000 in ESI tax offsets in total during any particular income year.

[94] ITAA 1997 s 360-15(2).

[95] ITAA 1997 ss 360-15(2), 360-30. A trustee that is assessed and liable to pay tax on the net income of a trust estate under ss 98, 99, 99A of the ITAA 1997 can also claim the tax offset: s 360-15(3). The amount of the tax offset in this case is the amount that the trustee would have been entitled to if it was an individual, less any amounts to which the members of the trust are entitled to under s 360-15(2): s 360-35.

[96] ITAA 1997 s 360(2). The trustee or partnership must give the member written notice of the determination with information that enables them to work out the amount of their tax offset. Written notice must be given within 3 months after the end of an income year: s 360-30(4).

[97] ITAA 1997 s 360-30(3).

[98] Treasury Laws Amendment (2018 Measures No. 2) Bill 2018 (Cth) cl 9 of Schedule 2 of Part 2 (proposed s 360-20(1A)).

[99] Explanatory Memorandum, Treasury Laws Amendment (2018 Measures No. 2) Bill 2018 (Cth) 2.46.

Example
Julian is a sophisticated investor who is one of five partners in a partnership. The partnership has invested $5 million in Zeta Co, which is an ESIC, in the 2018–19 income year. If the partnership was an individual, it would be entitled to a $200,000 tax offset for its investment in Zeta Co. Instead, this tax offset flows through to the partners. Julian is therefore entitled to a $40,000 tax offset (i.e., 1/5 of $200,000) in the 2018–19 income year.

Julian is also a member of a trust ('Trust 1') that has made a $1 million investment in Eta Co, which is also an ESIC, in the 2018–19 income year. If the trust was an individual, it would be entitled to a $200,000 tax offset for its investments in Eta Co. Instead, this tax offset flows through to the beneficiaries. The trustee determines that Julian is entitled to receive 50% of the tax offset. Julian is entitled to a $100,000 tax offset (i.e., 50% of $200,000) in the current income year.

Julian is also a member of another trust ('Trust 2') that has invested $450,000 in Theta Co, which is also an ESIC, in the 2018–19 income year. If the trust was an individual, it would be entitled to a $90,000 tax offset. The trustee determines that Julian is entitled to receive 90% of the tax offset. This would mean his total tax offset for 2018–19 is $221,000 ($40,000 + $100,000 + $81,000). However, under the proposed single combined limit, his total tax offset for the 2018–19 income year would be capped at $200,000.

The flow-through nature of the tax offset means that the limited partners in ESVCLPs that subscribe for shares in ESICs are currently entitled to a share of the ESI tax offset. Where this occurs, the limited partners benefit not only from the 20% ESI tax offset but also from the 10% ESVCLP tax offset.[100] This means that where the capital invested in an ESVCLP is applied to make an underlying investment in an ESIC, the limited partners receive two tax offsets in relation to what is effectively the same contribution. In order to address this windfall benefit, the Government is proposing to remove the flow-through of the ESI tax offset available to partners in ESVCLPs.[101] The proposed change does not affect members of VCLPs that invest in ESICs because they do not receive a double benefit since they are not entitled to any tax offset for their contributions to a VCLP. In any event, the reality is that ESIC investments will generally be far too underdeveloped to attract the attention of most VCLPs.[102]

---

[100] ITAA 1997 ss 61-760, 61-765. As mentioned above at 3.4, the ESVCP tax offset was introduced at the same time as the ESI program.

[101] Treasury Laws Amendment (2018 Measures No. 2) Bill 2018 (Cth) cls 5, 7 of Schedule 2 of Part 2 (proposed ss 360-15(1)(ia), 360-15(2)).

[102] As discussed at 3.4, VCLPs can invest in companies and unit trusts valued at up to $250 million, and are not limited to purchasing new equity. On the other hand, ESVCLPs can only invest in companies and unit trusts valued at up to $50 million, and must generally purchase new equity.

4.4 Modified CGT Treatment

Section 360-50 provides that an investor who is entitled to a tax offset in relation to the issue of shares in an ESIC is deemed to hold those shares on capital account and is subject to modified CGT treatment in relation to the shares. Interestingly, although the entitlement to modified CGT treatment is contingent on the entitlement to the tax offset, the tax offset cap of $200,000 does not limit the shares that qualify for modified CGT treatment.[103] In other words, an investor who pays more than $1 million for ESIC shares will only be entitled to a $200,000 tax offset, but they will receive modified CGT treatment on all their ESIC shares. This may be contrasted with the position relating to retail investors who invest more than $50,000 in ESIC shares in an income year. These investors are not subject to modified CGT treatment as they are not entitled to a tax offset since they have exceeded the retail investor cap.[104]

By deeming an investor to hold their shares on capital account, no general income tax issues will arise on the acquisition and disposal of their shares. This means that the investor will not be at risk of being treated as a 'share trader' who would be required to include the proceeds from the sale of their shares in assessable income under s 6-5 of the ITAA 1997 and be entitled to deductions for the cost of acquiring their shares under s 8-1 of the ITAA 1997. Instead, the investor will simply be taxed on their gains and losses under the CGT provisions in Parts 3-1 and 3-3 of the ITAA 1997 as modified by Subdivision 360-A.

The modified CGT treatment under Subdivision 360-A provides investors with special exemptions that operate as follows:

- an investor *may* disregard a capital gain arising from a CGT event happening to the shares if the investor has continuously held the shares since their issue, and the CGT event occurs on or after the first anniversary, but before the tenth anniversary of the issue;[105] and
- an investor *must* disregard a capital loss arising from a CGT event happening to the shares if the investor has continuously held the shares since their issue, and the CGT event occurs before the tenth anniversary of the issue.[106]

While many ESIC investments might be too small for most venture capital funds, it is more likely that ESVCLPs rather than VCLPs would make such investments.

[103] Australian Taxation Office, *Tax Incentives for Early Stage Investors* (n 92). The Explanatory Memorandum explains that this is because the relevant test is whether the investor has an 'entitlement' to claim the tax offset in relation to certain shares, not whether it actually does so: *ESI Explanatory Memorandum* (n 2) 1.11.

[104] Australian Taxation Office, *Tax Incentives for Early Stage Investors* (n 92).

[105] ITAA 1997 s 360-50(4).

[106] ITAA 1997 s 360-50(3). By requiring an entity to have continuously held the shares since their issue, the Government has ensured that only new shares issued by an ESIC will be eligible for the exemptions. Once the shares have been sold to a third party, the third party does not benefit from the exemptions. This is appropriate as the third party has not contributed capital to the ESIC, so there is no policy rationale for providing them with any exemptions.

The exemptions cease to apply where the shares have been continuously held by the investor for ten or more years. In this situation, the cost base and reduced cost base of the investor's shares are adjusted. Where an investor has continuously held the shares since their issue, the first element of their cost base and reduced cost base becomes, on the tenth anniversary of their issue, the market value of the shares at that time.[107] This ensures that only incremental gains or losses in value that occur *after* 10 years will be taken into account for CGT purposes.

The way that the modified CGT treatment applies over time is set out in Table 4.2.

It should be noted that where investors make capital gains in relation to ESIC shares that have been held for more than 10 years, these gains will usually qualify as 'discount capital gains' under the standard CGT rules.[108] This generally means that investors that are individuals or trusts can reduce their capital gains by 50%, while investors that are trustees of complying superannuation funds can reduce their capital gains by $33\frac{1}{3}\%$.[109]

A special rule provides that where a partnership holds shares in an ESIC, the modified CGT rules apply in relation to each partner's interests in such shares.[110]

Table 4.2 Modified CGT treatment under the ESI program

Period shares held	Capital gains	Capital losses
<12 months	Investor may not disregard capital gains arising in relation to the shares	Investor must disregard capital losses arising in relation to the shares
≥12 months but <10 years	Investor may disregard capital gains arising in relation to the shares	Investor must disregard capital losses arising in relation to the shares
≥10 years	Investor is subject to CGT in relation to capital gains and losses arising in relation to the shares. However, the first element of the cost base or reduced cost base of the shares will be deemed to be the market value of the shares on the tenth anniversary of the issue of the shares.	

[107] ITAA 1997 s 360-50(5).

[108] ITAA 1997 Division 115. Note that for a capital gain to qualify as a discount capital gain the requirements of ss 115-10, 115-15, 115-20 and 115-25 must be satisfied: s 115-5. In particular, note that a company is not entitled to any discount on a capital gain as it is not included on the list of entities mentioned in s 115-10.

[109] ITAA 1997 s 115-100. Note that investors are only entitled to the reductions under Division 115 on so much of their discount capital gains that remain after any capital losses and carry forward losses have first been applied against their capital gains: s 102-5.

[110] ITAA 1997 s 360-55(1), (2). This recognises that partners have separate CGT assets under the CGT regime, being their interests in the relevant assets of their partnerships. If ESIC shares have been held continuously by the partnership since their issue, on the tenth anniversary of the issue, the first element of the cost base or reduced cost base for the partner's interest in the shares becomes so much of the shares' market value on that anniversary as is calculated by reference to the partnership agreement (or partnership law if there is no agreement): s 360-55(3).

Special rules also ensure that the modified CGT treatment works appropriately with various roll-over provisions under the CGT regime, including same-asset roll-overs,[111] replacement-asset roll-overs,[112] roll-overs about wholly-owned companies[113] and scrip-for-scrip rollovers.[114]

Because the exemptions provided under the ESI program apply to both capital gains and capital losses, they can have either a beneficial or detrimental effect on investors. Presumably, the rationale for exempting both gains and losses is to achieve sym-

[111] A same-asset roll-over allows an entity to disregard a capital gain or loss made from disposing of a CGT asset to, or creating a CGT asset in, another entity: ITAA 1997 ss 112-140, 995-1. Examples of same-asset roll-overs include: the transfer of a CGT asset from one spouse to another because of a relationship breakdown; the transfer of a CGT asset of a trust to a company under a trust restructure; and the transfer of a CGT asset between certain related companies: s 112-150. Where a same-asset roll-over occurs, the modified CGT treatment provided under the ESI program is generally not affected (although note that some same-asset rollovers instead constitute roll-overs about wholly-owned companies). The new asset is treated as though it was the original asset (i.e., as though it was issued at the same time as the original asset and held for the same amount time as the original asset): s 360-60(1), (2), Division 122.

[112] A replacement-asset roll-over involves an entity's ownership of an original CGT asset ending, and the acquisition of a replacement asset. The roll-over allows the entity to defer the making of a capital gain or loss from this CGT event until a later CGT event happens: ITAA 1997 ss 112-105, 995-1. Examples of replacement-asset roll-overs include: an exchange of shares in the same company; an exchange of rights or options to acquire shares in a company; an exchange of shares in one company for shares in an interposed company; and an exchange of units in a unit trust for shares in a company: s 112-115. Where a replacement-asset roll-over occurs, the modified CGT treatment provided under the ESI tax incentive is generally not affected – the replacement asset is treated, for the purposes of the tax incentive, as though it was the original asset (although note that some same-asset rollovers instead constitute roll-overs about wholly-owned companies or scrip-for-scrip roll-overs): s 360-60(1), (2), Division 122, Subdivision 124-M.

[113] A roll-over in relation to a wholly-owned company can occur when a special 'trigger events' happens. Examples of trigger events include: an individual disposes of a CGT asset to a wholly-owned company; all the partners in a partnership dispose of their interests in a CGT asset of the partnership to a wholly-owned company; an individual, trustee or all the partners in a partnership create contractual or other rights in a wholly-owned company; or an individual, trustee or all the partners in a partnership grant an option to a wholly-owned company: ITAA 1997 ss 122-15, 122-125. Different consequences apply depending on which trigger event occurs; however, generally speaking, the roll-over allows an entity to disregard the capital gains or losses they make from the trigger event or disposal: see ss 122-40, 122-45, 122-65. If a relevant trigger event occurs in relation to shares in an ESIC that have been continuously held by an entity since their issue, and the trigger event gives rise to a roll-over that occurs after the first anniversary, but before the tenth anniversary of the issue of the shares, then the first element of the cost base and reduced cost base of the shares just before the roll-over is taken to be their market value at that time: s 360-65.

[114] A scrip-for-scrip roll-over applies in relation to certain complicated arrangements where an entity exchanges a share in one company for a share in another company, often as a result of a corporate take-over: ITAA 1997 s 124-780(1). There are a number of conditions that need to be met in order for the roll-over to apply: s 124-780. Normally, if a scrip-for-scrip roll-over applies, then a capital gain made from the original share is generally disregarded and the first element of the cost base of the new share becomes, broadly speaking, the cost base of the original share: s 124-785. However, when a scrip-for-scrip rollover applies in relation to a continuously held share in an ESIC, and the rollover occurs after the first anniversary, but before the tenth anniversary of the issue of the share, the first element of the cost base and reduced cost base of the share just before the roll-over is taken to be its market value at that time: s 360-65.

metrical treatment.[115] This is consistent with the treatment that applies to gains and losses arising under the VCLP and ESVCLP programs (see 3.4).[116] However, it needs to be pointed out that this treatment operates as a 'double-edged sword' and actually punishes ESIC investors that have made losses as a result of taking risks, which seems contrary to the policy intent of the tax incentive. The irony is that investors that have made losses in ESICs will actually be worse off than investors that have made losses in other companies, as those other investors will be able to claim their losses.[117]

Example
Jackie is a sophisticated investor. On 1 August 2018, Jackie invests $200,000 in Iota Co, which is an ESIC. Jackie is entitled to claim a tax offset of $40,000 (i.e., 20% of $200,000) in respect of her investment in the 2018–19 income year.

If Jackie sells the Iota Co shares 8 years later for $600,000, she can disregard the $400,000 capital gain that she has made.

However, if Jackie sells the Iota Co shares 14 years later for $2 million, she will be subject to CGT. Assuming that the market value of the Iota Co shares on 1 August 2028 was $1.8 million, Jackie will make a capital gain of $200,000 in the 2032–33 income year.

4.5 Reporting Obligations

To assist the ATO in administering the ESI program, ESICs are required to comply with special third party reporting rules contained in Subdivision 396-B of Schedule 1 to the TAA.[118] In simple terms, these rules place obligations on a company to provide information in the approved form about shares it has issued during a financial year that could give rise to an entitlement to the tax offset or modified CGT treatment for an investor under Subdivision 360-A.[119] The Government has stated that

[115] It should be noted that while shares need to be held for at least one year in order for an investor to be able to disregard capital gains, there is no corresponding period for capital losses. This means that the treatment of gains and losses is not entirely symmetrical. In any event, the reality is that most investors will probably find it very difficult to dispose of their shares in such a short time frame given the illiquid nature of the investment.

[116] See ITAA 1997 ss 118-405, 118-407.

[117] Under the CGT regime, taxpayers can only offset their capital losses against their capital gains: ITAA 1997 s 102-5.

[118] The third party reporting rules are an important part of the overall administrative architecture of the tax system and are designed to assist the ATO with the identification, collection or recovery of tax related liabilities. They do not just apply to ESICs, but also a range of other entities in relation to specific kinds of transactions.

[119] TAA s 396-55 (item 10 in the table). The approved form is available through the ATO's business portal and requires information to be provided concerning: the investor's ABN, name and address; the number of new shares issued to the investor in the company; the amount paid for the new shares; the date the shares were issued; and the percentage of shares in the company held by the investor immediately after the shares were issued. The information must be provided on or before the 31st day after the end of the financial year or such other time as the Commissioner specifies by legislative instrument.

this approach 'minimises compliance costs for all parties involved by requiring the reporting of only the minimum amount of information necessary for the ATO to effectively administer the regime'.[120] The information collected from ESICs helps the ATO to 'minimise opportunities for entities to inappropriately claim the tax offset and provide sufficient information to assure the Government that the measure remains appropriately targeted and effective'.[121]

4.6 Diagrams Illustrating the Operation of the ESI Program

By way of summary, Figs. 4.2 and 4.3 illustrate the basic operation of the ESI program in situations where an investment in an ESIC is made directly by an individual and indirectly through a partnership.

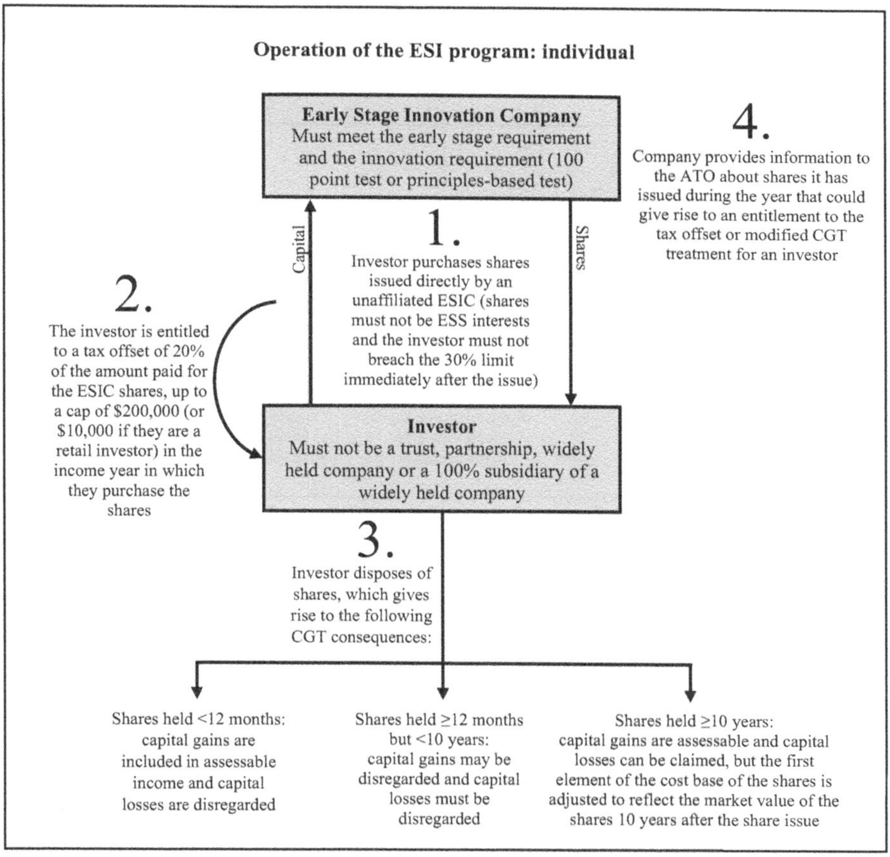

Fig. 4.2 Operation of the ESI program: individual

[120] *ESI Explanatory Memorandum* (n 2) 1.15.

[121] Ibid 1.130.

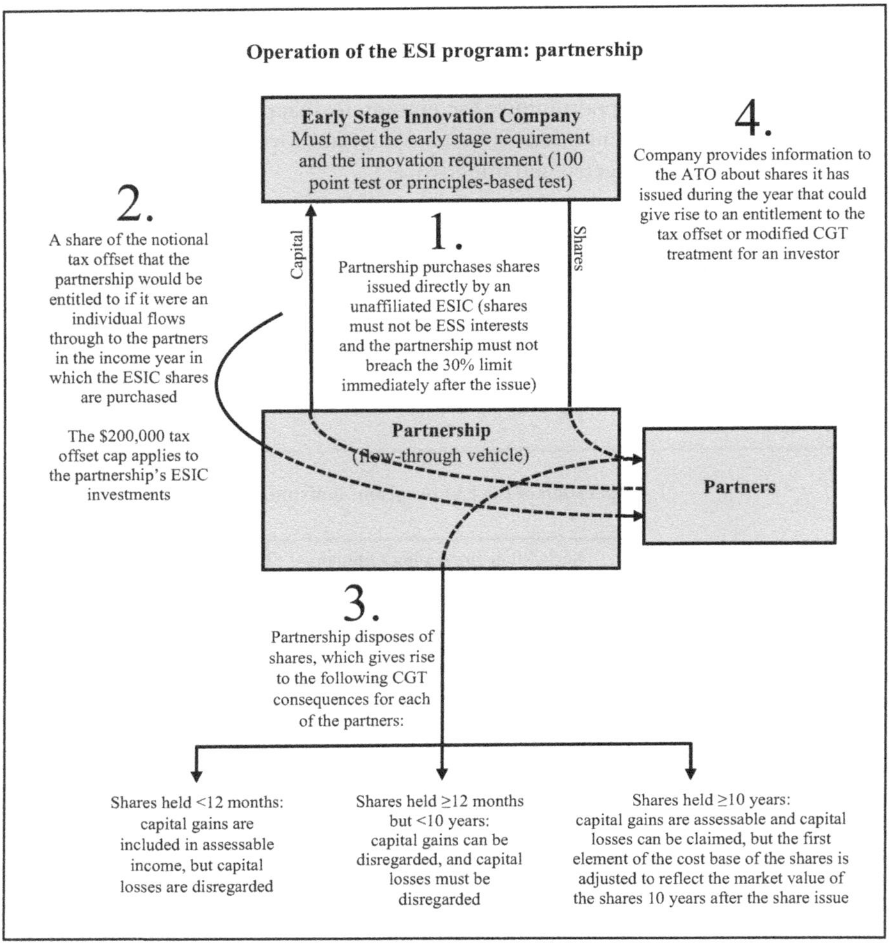

Fig. 4.3 Operation of the ESI program: partnership

4.7 Conclusion

This Chapter has examined the ESI program in detail, setting out the policy considerations that motivated its introduction and design, and the special niche that it occupies alongside Australia's other venture capital tax incentive programs. It is interesting to note that while the ESI program has been in operation for just over two years, very little data on the program has been released to the public. This has attracted criticism from some commentators,[122] with advocacy group StartupAUS

[122] Denham Sadler, *Shocking Lack of Angel Investor Data* (7 December 2017) InnovationAus.com, <https://www.innovationaus.com/2017/12/Shocking-lack-of-angel-investor-data>.

raising 'concerns over the lack of transparency around the scheme'.[123] It has nevertheless been reported that in the 2016–17 income year, approximately 3,400 investors invested around $300 million in 340 ESICs.[124] While it is acknowledged that the ESI program is still relatively new and is not yet likely to have achieved many measurable outcomes, it would be appropriate for data on the program's uptake to be made available to the public in the future so that its impact can be analysed and evaluated.[125] This would help ensure that the program stays on track to meet its policy objectives. In this regard, it is interesting to note that ISA regularly releases information on the ESVCLP and VCLP programs, including details of the number of registered funds and their committed capital,[126] as well as details of the number of investees, their sizes and the sectors in which they operate.[127] This information is deidentified in order to protect the privacy of investors and investees, but nevertheless provides a big-picture snapshot of the progress of these programs. Adopting a similar approach in relation to the ESI program would be useful and welcome.

References

Auditor-General, 'Design and Monitoring of the National Innovation and Science Agenda' (Performance Audit No. 10, Australian National Audit Office, 2017)

Australian Accounting Standards Board, 'Framework for the Preparation and Presentation of Financial Statements' (Framework, 2004)

Australian Government, *Entrepreneurs' Programme* (10 December 2018) Business.gov.au, <https://www.business.gov.au/assistance/entrepreneurs-programme-summary>

Australian Government, 'Tax Expenditures Statement 2017' (Statement, 2018)

Australian Government, 'Tax Incentives for Early Stage Investors' (Policy Discussion Paper, 2016)

Australian Taxation Office, 'A Step-by-Step Guide to the Principles-Based Innovation Test' (2017)

Australian Taxation Office, *Class Rulings System*, CR 2001/1, 28 February 2001 (consolidated ruling 11 September 2013)

Australian Taxation Office, 'Eligibility of Accelerator Programs Under the 100-Point Innovation Test' (2017)

Australian Taxation Office, *ESIC Decision Tool* (22 June 2017) <https://www.ato.gov.au/Calculators-and-tools/ESIC-decision-tool/>

Australian Taxation Office, *For Investors* (2 August 2017) <https://www.ato.gov.au/Business/Tax-incentives-for-innovation/In-detail/Tax-incentives-for-early-stage-investors/?page=4#For_investors>

---

[123] StartupAUS, 'Crossroads: An Action Plan to Develop a World-Leading Tech Startup Ecosystem in Australia' (2017) 67.

[124] Paul Colgan, 'Tax Breaks Drew $300 Million in Investment for Australian Startups in a Single Year', *Business Insider Australia*, 28 February 2018 <https://www.businessinsider.com.au/startup-investment-australia-impact-of-tax-breaks-2018-2>.

[125] The cost of the ESI program is already reported in the Government's annual tax expenditure statements. It is estimated to be around $65 million for each of the 2017–18 to 2020–21 income years: Australian Government, 'Tax Expenditures Statement 2017' (Statement, 2018) 66.

[126] See e.g., Innovation and Science Australia, 'Annual Report 2017–18' (Annual Report, 2018).

[127] Department of Industry, Innovation and Science, *Venture Capital Dashboard* (September 2018) <https://www.industry.gov.au/data-and-publications/venture-capital-dashboard>.

Australian Taxation Office, 'Issue: 3-Year Expense Test and Expenditure Incurred After the Test Time in Tax Incentives for Early Stage Company Investors' (Discussion Paper, 2017)
Australian Taxation Office, 'Issue: Do the Early Stage Innovation Tests Need to be Satisfied by the Company that Issues Shares to Investors?' (Discussion Paper, 2017)
Australian Taxation Office, 'Issue: Meaning of the Phrase "Incurred Total Expenses" in the Early Stage Innovation Company Tests' (Discussion Paper, 2017)
Australian Taxation Office, 'Issue: When Must a Company be a 100% Subsidiary for its Income and Expenses to be Accounted for Under the ESIC "Early Stage" Tests?' (Discussion Paper, 2017)
Australian Taxation Office, *Let's Talk: Tax Incentives for Early Stage Investors* <https://lets-talk.ato.gov.au/ESIC>
Australian Taxation Office, *Principles-Based Innovation Test* (2 August 2017) <https://www.ato.gov.au/Business/Tax-incentives-for-innovation/In-detail/Tax-incentives-for-early-stage-investors/?page=3#Principles_based_innovation_test>
Australian Taxation Office, *Private Rulings*, TR 2006/11, 4 October 2006 (consolidated ruling 16 August 2017)
Australian Taxation Office, *Public Rulings*, TR 2006/10, 4 October 2006 (consolidated ruling 12 October 2016)
Australian Taxation Office, *Qualifying as an Early Stage Innovation Company* (2 August 2017) <https://www.ato.gov.au/Business/Tax-incentives-for-innovation/In-detail/Tax-incentives-for-early-stage-investors/?page=2#100_point_innovation_test_requirements>
Australian Taxation Office, *Tax Incentives for Early Stage Investors* (2 August 2017) <https://www.ato.gov.au/Business/Tax-incentives-for-innovation/In-detail/Tax-incentives-for-early-stage-investors/?page=1#The_sophisticated_investor_test>
Bailey, Michael, 'Early Stage Innovation Company Investor Tax Breaks Misunderstood', *Australian Financial Review* (online), 4 May 2017 <http://www.afr.com/leadership/entrepreneur/early-stage-innovation-company-investor-tax-breaks-misunderstood-by-founders-investors-20170504-gvyr4x#ixzz4idVpA5H7>
Brass, Jessica and Mark Trewhella, 'Early Stage Innovation Companies – A Deeper Dive' (2017) 51(8) *Taxation in Australia* 427
Business.gov.au, *Research Service Providers: Using a Research Service Provider (RSP) to Conduct R&D* (5 April 2018) <https://www.business.gov.au/assistance/research-and-development-tax-incentive/research-service-providers>
Coles Myer Finance Ltd v Federal Commissioner of Taxation (1993) 93 ATC 4214
Colgan, Paul, 'Tax Breaks Drew $300 Million in Investment for Australian Startups in a Single Year', *Business Insider Australia*, 28 February 2018 <https://www.businessinsider.com.au/startup-investment-australia-impact-of-tax-breaks-2018-2>
Corporations Act 2001 (Cth)
Corporations Regulations 2001 (Cth)
Department of Industry, Innovation and Science, 'Entrepreneurs' Programme – Programme Guidelines Version 10' (Programme Guidelines, December 2018)
Department of Industry, Innovation and Science, *Venture Capital Dashboard* (September 2018) <https://www.industry.gov.au/data-and-publications/venture-capital-dashboard>
Design Act 2003 (Cth)
Explanatory Memorandum, Tax Laws Amendment (Tax Incentives for Innovation) Bill 2016 (Cth)
Explanatory Memorandum, Treasury Laws Amendment (2018 Measures No. 2) Bill 2018 (Cth)
Explanatory Memorandum, Treasury Laws Amendment (Tax Integrity and Other Measures) Bill 2018 (Cth)
Financial Corporations Act 1974 (Cth)
Gioskos, Mark and Travis McCarthy, 'New Tax Incentives for Investors in Start-Up Companies' (2017) 51(7) *Taxation in Australia* 370

Gouveia, Carlos, *Early Stage Innovation Companies – 10 Months On* (27 April 2017) Colin Biggers & Paisley Lawyers <https://www.cbp.com.au/insights/2017/april/early-stage-innovation-companies-10-months-on>

Higher Education Funding Act 1988 (Cth)

Income Tax Assessment Act 1936 (Cth)

Income Tax Assessment Act 1997 (Cth)

Industry Research and Development Act 1986 (Cth)

Innovation and Science Australia, 'Annual Report 2017–18' (Annual Report, 2018)

IP Australia, *PBR Basics* (19 April 2018) <https://www.ipaustralia.gov.au/plant-breeders-rights/understanding-pbr>

IP Australia, *Phasing out of the Innovation Patent System* <https://www.ipaustralia.gov.au/policy-register/phasing-out-of-the-innovation-patent-system>

IP Australia, *Registration and Certification* (3 March 2016) <https://www.ipaustralia.gov.au/designs/understanding-designs/registration-and-certification>

IP Australia, *Types of Patents* (30 May 2016) <https://www.ipaustralia.gov.au/patents/understanding-patents/types-patents>

Misic, Dragan, 'New Approach to Capital Raising: Tax Perspective' (2017) 21(2) *The Tax Specialist* 65

Nilsen Development Laboratories Pty Ltd v Federal Commissioner of Taxation (1981) 81 ATC 4031

OECD, *OSLO Manual: Guidelines for Collecting and Interpreting Innovation Data* (OECD, 3rd ed, 2005)

Patents Act 1990 (Cth)

Phillips, Michael, *Tax Incentives for Investors in Early Stage Investment Companies* (18 May 2016) Swaab <http://www.swaab.com.au/Publications/Publications/Tax-Incentives-for-Investors-in-Early-Stage-Invest?utm_source=Mondaq&utm_medium=syndication&utm_campaign=View-Original>

Plant Breeder's Rights Act 1994 (Cth)

Sadler, Denham, *Shocking Lack of Angel Investor Data* (7 December 2017) InnovationAus.com <https://www.innovationaus.com/2017/12/Shocking-lack-of-angel-investor-data>

StartupAUS, *Crossroads: An Action Plan to Develop a World-Leading Tech Startup Ecosystem in Australia* (Report, 2017)

Tax Administration Act 1953 (Cth)

Treasury Laws Amendment (2018 Measures No. 2) Bill 2018 (Cth)

Treasury Laws Amendment (Making Sure Multinationals Pay Their Fair Share of Tax in Australia and Other Measures) Bill 2018 (Cth)

Treasury Laws Amendment (Tax Integrity and Other Measures) Bill 2018 (Cth)

UNSW Australia Business School, *The Role and Performance of Accelerators in the Australian Startup Ecosystem* (Final Report for the Department of Industry, Innovation and Science, 2016)

Woellner, R, S Barkoczy, S Murphy, C Evans and D Pinto, *Australian Taxation Law* (Oxford University Press, 28th ed, 2018)

Chapter 5
United Kingdom's Seed Enterprise Investment Scheme

Abstract As mentioned in Chap. 1, the United Kingdom has developed its own angel tax incentive program, known as the Seed Enterprise Investment Scheme (SEIS). The SEIS was introduced in 2012 and is designed to help small, high-risk companies raise equity capital by offering tax incentives to individuals who subscribe for ordinary shares in them. While Australia's ESI program discussed in Chap. 4 was loosely modelled on the SEIS, the programs have a number of significant differences. For instance, although both programs target investments in small early stage companies, they contain quite different eligibility criteria. The SEIS, for example, focuses on criteria such as a company's gross assets and the number of its employees, whereas the ESI program focuses on criteria such as a company's expenses and assessable income. The SEIS also contains a blacklist of 'excluded activities' that an investee company must not carry on, whereas the ESI program does not have such a list. In addition, while the ESI program uses a 'point-in-time' test to determine whether a company qualifies as an ESIC, several SEIS requirements are 'ongoing', meaning that if they cease to be met during the relevant period, tax benefits that have been granted to investors may be withdrawn. Another key difference between the programs is that the SEIS does not require investee companies to meet any specific 'innovation requirements' like the ones that exist under the ESI program. There are also important differences in the nature of the tax incentives provided under the programs. While both the SEIS and the ESI program use a combination of front-end and back-end tax incentives to encourage angel investment, the SEIS provides a broader range of tax incentives than the ESI program. This chapter closely examines the SEIS and compares and contrasts it with the ESI program as well as Australia's formal venture capital tax incentive programs discussed in Chap. 3. The comparative discussion in this chapter is then used to inform the suggestions we make for reforms to the ESI program in Chap. 6.

S. Barkoczy, T. Wilkinson, *Incentivising Angels*, SpringerBriefs in Law,
https://doi.org/10.1007/978-981-13-6632-1_5

5.1 Background

The United Kingdom introduced the SEIS in 2012.[1] Like Australia's ESI program (discussed in Chap. 4), the SEIS is a highly regulated tax incentive program that aims to encourage angel investment in start-ups. The SEIS provides tax relief for amounts subscribed by individuals for shares in a company that meets specified requirements.[2] In order for an investment to attract tax relief, a special 'risk-to-capital condition' must be met in relation to the relevant share issue (see 5.2).[3] In addition, the investor must be a 'qualifying investor' in relation to the shares (see 5.3)[4] and a number of 'general requirements' must be met in respect of the shares (see 5.4).[5] Finally, the company that issues the shares must be a 'qualifying company' (see 5.5).[6]

The SEIS provides investors with generous front-end and back-end tax incentives that have certain broad similarities with those available under the ESI program (see 5.6 and 5.7). The SEIS, however, also provides special loss and reinvestment reliefs (see 5.8 and 5.9), which do not exist under the ESI program.

The SEIS operates alongside two much older United Kingdom venture capital tax incentive programs: the Enterprise Investment Scheme (which was introduced in 1994) and the Venture Capital Trusts scheme (which was introduced in 1995). The Venture Capital Trusts scheme is a formal venture capital program that provides tax incentives to entities that invest in specially regulated companies known as 'Venture Capital Trusts'.[7] The Enterprise Investment Scheme, on the other hand, provides tax incentives primarily to encourage informal venture capital investment.[8]

---

[1] The SEIS was introduced by the *Finance Act 2012* (UK), which amended the *Income Tax Act 2007* (UK) ('ITA 2007 (UK)').

[2] ITA 2007 (UK) ss 257A, 257AA.

[3] ITA 2007 (UK) s 257AAA.

[4] An investor will be a qualifying investor if they meet the requirements set out in Chapter 2 of Part 5A of the ITA 2007 (UK): s 257B.

[5] The general requirements are set out in Chapter 3 of Part 5A of the ITA 2007 (UK): s 257C.

[6] A company will be a qualifying company if it meets the requirements set out in Chapter 4 of Part 5A of the ITA 2007 (UK): s 257D.

[7] Venture Capital Trusts must be approved by HM Revenue & Customs to operate as formal venture capital funds. They invest in (or make loans to) underlying investee companies, which must be unlisted (among other things). Investors in Venture Capital Trusts can receive front-endincome tax relief for the purchase of shares in a Venture Capital Trust and back-end CGT relief in relation to gains they make on their investments: HM Revenue & Customs, 'Tax Relief for Investors Using Venture Capital Schemes' (Guidance, 3 October 2018) <https://www.gov.uk/guidance/venture-capital-schemes-tax-relief-for-investors>. See also HM Revenue & Customs, 'Venture Capital Schemes Manual: Venture Capital Trusts: Contents' (HMRC Internal Manual, 16 October 2018) <https://www.gov.uk/hmrc-internal-manuals/venture-capital-schemes-manual/vcm50000>.

[8] The Enterprise Investment Scheme provides a range of tax incentives to individuals who invest in small, high-risk companies. The scheme offers up-front income tax relief, back-end CGT and loss relief, and CGT deferrals where capital gains are reinvested under the scheme: HM Revenue & Customs, 'Tax Relief for Investors Using Venture Capital Schemes' (n 7). See also HM Revenue & Customs, 'Use the Enterprise Investment Scheme (EIS) to Raise Money for Your Company'

The SEIS is closely modelled on the Enterprise Investment Scheme.[9] Both schemes are intended to help small, high-risk companies raise equity capital by offering tax incentives to investors who invest in them. The SEIS, however, specifically targets companies that might not otherwise attract sufficient venture capital investment under the Enterprise Investment Scheme due to their very early stage of development. The SEIS therefore has tighter eligibility criteria than the Enterprise Investment Scheme in that it specifically targets smaller and newer companies.[10] Recognising the particular capital raising difficulties that these companies face, the SEIS provides more generous tax incentives than those available under the Enterprise Investment Scheme.[11]

While Australia's ESI program is loosely modelled on the SEIS, it will become evident from the following discussion that the two programs have many significant differences. This chapter examines the SEIS and compares and contrasts it with the ESI program as well as Australia's formal venture capital tax incentive programs (discussed in Chap. 3).

(Guidance, 12 October 2018) <https://www.gov.uk/guidance/venture-capital-schemes-apply-for-the-enterprise-investment-scheme>. The Enterprise Investment Scheme also allows for managed 'EIS investment funds' to be formed, which make investments on behalf of individuals. In this respect, the scheme possesses some of the features of a formal venture capital program: see further HM Revenue & Customs, 'Venture Capital Schemes Manual: EIS: Income Tax Relief: Supplementary and General: Approved Investment Fund as Nominee' (HMRC Internal Manual, 16 October 2018) <https://www.gov.uk/hmrc-internal-manuals/venture-capital-schemes-manual/vcm16050>.

[9] The similarities between the two schemes were viewed positivity by some commentators, one of whom noted that companies can raise capital through the SEIS before moving on to raising capital through the Enterprise Investment Scheme or Venture Capital Trust scheme 'without the need for two separate sets of rules': Andrew Harper, 'Finance Act Notes: Section 38 and Schedule 6: Seed Enterprise Investment Scheme' (2012) 4 *British Tax Review* 407, 410. This is also beneficial for the tax system, as it avoids the complexity of introducing a wholly independent third scheme: at 410.

[10] For instance, companies under the SEIS must have fewer gross assets and employees than those under the Enterprise Investment Scheme, they are significantly more limited in how much investment they may receive through 'risk capital schemes' (e.g., venture capital incentives) and they can only have been trading for two years or less (whereas companies under the Enterprise Investment Scheme have much more lax age requirements): see ITA 2007 (UK) ss 173A, 175A, 186, 186A, 257 DC, 257DL, 257DI, 257DJ, 257HF. The fact that the SEIS targets smaller and newer companies explains why it is called the 'Seed' Enterprise Investment Scheme.

[11] HM Revenue & Customs, 'Enterprise Investment Scheme and Seed Enterprise Investment Scheme April 2017 Statistics on Companies Raising Funds' (Official Statistics Release, 27 April 2017) <https://www.gov.uk/government/uploads/system/uploads/attachment_data/file/611524/April_2017_Commentary_EIS_SEIS_Official_Statistics_v5.pdf>. The rate of income tax relief available under the SEIS is 50% of the invested amount, compared to 30% under the Enterprise Investment Scheme. However, it should be noted that investors can invest greater amounts under the Enterprise Investment Scheme (up to £2 million in certain circumstances, compared to £100,000 under the SEIS): HM Revenue & Customs, 'Tax Relief for Investors Using Venture Capital Schemes' (n 7).

5.2 The Risk-To-Capital Condition

As mentioned above, a range of requirements must be satisfied in order for an issue of shares to attract tax relief under the SEIS. The first of these is the recently introduced 'risk-to-capital condition', which functions as a gateway requirement that must be met before any other requirements are considered.[12] The risk-to-capital condition is met in relation to an investment if, having regard to the circumstances existing at the time of the share issue, it is reasonable to conclude that the investee company has objectives to grow and develop its trade in the long-term, and there is a significant risk that there will be a loss of capital of an amount greater than the net investment return to investors.[13] The risk-to-capital condition was introduced in 2018 in order to exclude 'tax-motivated investments' from receiving support.[14] It is designed to ensure that investee companies under the SEIS are 'genuine entrepreneurial businesses' that fall 'within the spirit' of the SEIS.[15] In other words, it is aimed at ensuring that investments made under the SEIS are legitimate venture capital investments.

From a comparative perspective, it is worth noting that investments made under Australia's VCLP and ESVCLP programs are also required to be held 'at-risk' (see 3.4).[16] There are, however, no at-risk requirements prescribed under the ESI program.

5.3 Investor Requirements

Under the SEIS only individuals are entitled to tax relief.[17] This contrasts with the ESI program, which provides tax incentives not only to individuals, but also to certain other entities, such as companies and trustees of superannuation funds (see 4.3).

---

[12] The risk to capital condition applies from 15 March 2018 and corresponding conditions also exist under the Enterprise Investment Scheme and the Venture Capital Trusts scheme: ITA 2007 (UK) ss 157A, 257AAA, 286ZA; HM Revenue & Customs, 'Venture Capital Schemes Manual: Risk-To-Capital Condition: An Overview of the Risk-To-Capital Condition' (HMRC Internal Manual, 16 October 2018) <https://www.gov.uk/hmrc-internal-manuals/venture-capital-schemes-manual/vcm8530>.

[13] ITA 2007 (UK) s 257AAA. The net investment return takes into account the value of SEIS tax relief received by the investor.

[14] HM Revenue & Customs, 'Income Tax: Venture Capital Schemes – Risk to Capital Condition' (Policy Paper, 22 November 2017) <https://www.gov.uk/government/publications/income-tax-venture-capital-schemes-risk-to-capital-condition/income-tax-venture-capital-schemes-risk-to-capital-condition>.

[15] Ibid. It has been noted that 'companies that are comfortably in line with the stated purpose of the venture capital schemes should meet the risk-to-capital condition': HM Revenue & Customs, 'Venture Capital Schemes Manual: Risk-To-Capital Condition: An Overview of the Risk-To-Capital Condition' (n 12).

[16] ITAA 1997 ss 118-425(1), 118-427(1).

[17] ITA 2007 (UK) s 257AA. Tax relief may also be available where an individual subscribes for and holds shares through a nominee: s 257HE. This exception does not, however, allow investors to

The SEIS does not allow individuals to be employees of an investee company (unless they are also directors, in which case they are not treated as employees).[18] In addition, investors must not have a 'substantial interest' in the company from the time when it is incorporated to immediately before the third anniversary of the share issue.[19] An investor will have a substantial interest where they own more than 30% of the company's issued share capital, its voting rights or rights to its assets on winding up.[20] This requirement has similarities with the 30% requirement under the ESI program (see 4.3). A key difference between the two requirements, however, is that the SEIS requirement is an ongoing requirement, while the requirement under the ESI program only needs to be met at the test time. Because the 30% requirement under the SEIS is ongoing, it may be difficult for investors to make follow-on investments in their investee companies (at least until three years have passed) without losing or reducing their entitlement to the SEIS tax relief (see 5.6).

There are also a range of special SEIS requirements that are designed to maintain the integrity of the program and prevent its misuse. Investors under the SEIS must not subscribe for shares pursuant to a reciprocal arrangement where another person subscribes for shares in another company in which the investor (or any other individual who is party to the arrangement) has a substantial interest.[21] Furthermore, from the time when the investee company is incorporated until three years after the share issue, no person may make a 'linked loan' (i.e., a loan that would not have been made, or would have been made on different terms, if the investor had not subscribed for the shares) to the investor.[22] Finally, the shares must be subscribed for

---

obtain income tax relief if they invest in a partnership which in turn invests in shares (because the individual would own a proportion of all the partnership assets rather than having sole ownership of a specific allocation of shares): HM Revenue & Customs, 'Venture Capital Schemes Manual: SEIS: Income Tax Relief: Supplementary and General: Nominees and Bare Trustees' (HMRC Internal Manual, 16 October 2018) <https://www.gov.uk/hmrc-internal-manuals/venture-capital-schemes-manual/vcm37040>.

[18] ITA 2007 (UK) s 257BA; HM Revenue & Customs, 'Venture Capital Schemes Manual: SEIS: Income Tax Relief: The Investor: No Employee Investors' (HMRC Internal Manual, 16 October 2018) <https://www.gov.uk/hmrc-internal-manuals/venture-capital-schemes-manual/vcm32020>. The fact that directors who are also investors in a company are not treated as employees for the purposes of the SEIS is a sensible design feature that allows angels to play a role in managing their investee companies without affecting their entitlement to the tax incentives: European Commission, 'Effectiveness of Tax Incentives for Venture Capital and Business Angels to Foster the Investment of SMEs and Start-ups: Final Report' (Working Paper No 68, European Commission, June 2017) 77–8.

[19] ITA 2007 (UK) s 257BB. Harper notes that the claimed justification for the substantial interest rule is that the Government is 'keen to promote external investment in start-ups rather than reward founder capital', which is subsidised under another Government program known as 'Entrepreneurs' Relief': Andrew Harper, 'Finance Act Notes: Section 56: SEIS: Income Tax Relief; Section 57: SEIS: Re-Investment Relief' (2013) 4 *British Tax Review* 443, 446.

[20] ITA 2007 (UK) s 257BF.

[21] ITA 2007 (UK) s 257 BC.

[22] ITA 2007 (UK) s 257BD.

by the investor for genuine commercial reasons, and not as part of a scheme or arrangement the main purpose of which is the avoidance of tax.[23]

5.4 General Requirements

The general requirements under the SEIS apply primarily to the shares that are issued to an investor. These shares must be ordinary shares that are subscribed for wholly in cash and are fully paid up at the time they are issued.[24] They must be issued to raise money for the purpose of a 'qualifying business activity'[25] that is carried on by either the company or its 'qualifying 90% subsidiary',[26] and the money must be spent for this purpose within three years.[27] There must be no pre-arranged exits in place in relation to the shares,[28] they must be issued for genuine commercial reasons and not as part of a scheme or arrangement the main purpose of which is to avoid tax,[29] and they must not be issued in connection with certain 'disqualifying arrangements'.[30]

The general requirements under the SEIS differ markedly from the requirements under the ESI program. While both initiatives require the issue of shares, the ESI

---

[23] ITA 2007 (UK) s 257BE.

[24] ITA 2007 (UK) s 257CA. From the time when the shares are issued until the third anniversary of their issue, they must not carry any present or future preferential rights to dividends, to a company's assets on its winding up, or to be redeemed.

[25] A qualifying business activity can include a 'new qualifying trade' (see below), as well as R&D that the company is undertaking from which it is intended that a new qualifying trade will be derived: ITA 2007 (UK) s 257HG.

[26] A subsidiary is a qualifying 90% subsidiary of another company ('the relevant company') for the purposes of the SEIS where: the relevant company has at least 90% of the subsidiary's issued share capital and 90% of the voting power in the subsidiary; in the event of winding up or any other circumstances, the relevant company would be beneficially entitled to receive at least 90% of the subsidiary's assets which would then be available for distribution to equity holders of the subsidiary; the relevant company is beneficially entitled to receive at least 90% of any profits of the subsidiary which are available for distribution to equity holders of the subsidiary; no person other than the relevant company has control of the subsidiary; and no arrangements exist by virtue of which any of the above conditions would cease to be met: ITA 2007 (UK) ss 190, 257HJ.

[27] ITA 2007 (UK) ss 257 AC, 257CB, 257CC.

[28] ITA 2007 (UK) s 257CD.

[29] ITA 2007 (UK) s 257 CE.

[30] ITA 2007 (UK) s 257CF. The meaning of 'disqualifying arrangements' is set out in the relevant section. HM Revenue & Customs has noted that the purpose of this requirement is 'to prevent the schemes being used primarily for the purpose of delivering a tax mitigation product to investors with little or no other commercial purpose; or of delivering the benefits of tax-advantaged finance to another entity or project which would not itself qualify for support under the schemes or whose owners do not want to relinquish equity': HM Revenue & Customs, 'Venture Capital Schemes Manual: SEIS: Income Tax Relief: General Requirements: No Disqualifying Arrangements Requirement' (HMRC Internal Manual, 16 October 2018) <https://www.gov.uk/hmrc-internal-manuals/venture-capital-schemes-manual/vcm33080>.

program does not place any time limit on how or when money must be spent by investees, does not prohibit pre-arranged exits and does not contain any overarching internal anti-avoidance rules.[31]

5.5 Company Requirements

The SEIS requires an issuing company to meet two kinds of requirements: point-in-time requirements and ongoing requirements.[32] Point-in-time requirements (see 5.5.1) must be met at the time the company issues the shares (this is similar to the 'test time' requirement used under the ESI program). Ongoing requirements (see 5.5.2), on the other hand, must generally be met continuously over certain prescribed time periods. Ongoing requirements necessitate continued monitoring, meaning that they will generally impose a higher compliance and regulatory burden than point-in-time requirements.[33] Ongoing requirements also raise the potential that a tax incentive may be 'clawed back' from investors if a company's circumstances change so that the requirements are no longer met (see 5.6). This has the potential to create some uncertainty for investors.

5.5.1 Point-In-Time Requirements

The point-in-time requirements require an issuing company to:

- meet the 'financial health' requirement immediately after the share issue;[34]

[31] The ESI program nevertheless operates subject to the general anti-avoidance rules contained in Part IVA of the *Income Tax Assessment Act 1936* (Cth).

[32] The SEIS features an 'advance assurance' facility, whereby companies can receive guidance on whether they are likely to meet the SEIS requirements: HM Revenue & Customs, *Apply for Advance Assurance on a Venture Capital Scheme* (31 August 2018) Gov.uk <https://www.gov.uk/guidance/venture-capital-schemes-apply-for-advance-assurance>. Between the commencement of the SEIS in 2012 and March 2017, a reported 13,645 'Advance Assurance Applications' were received, of which approximately 85% were approved: HM Revenue & Customs, 'Enterprise Investment Scheme and Seed Enterprise Investment Scheme' (Statistics, April 2017) <https://www.gov.uk/government/uploads/system/uploads/attachment_data/file/611525/Combined_tables_to_publish.pdf>.

[33] As noted in Chapter 4, the ESI program does not have any ongoing requirements. The Australian Government has noted that ongoing activity checks would impose an unnecessary regulatory burden on ESICs and increase risk and uncertainty for investors: Explanatory Memorandum, Tax Laws Amendment (Tax Incentives for Innovation) Bill 2016 (Cth) 1.31–1.32.

[34] ITA 2007 (UK) s 257DE. The financial health requirement is that the issuing company must not be 'in difficulty'. A company is 'in difficulty' if it is reasonable to assume that it would be regarded as a firm in difficulty for the purposes of the *Community Guidelines on State Aid for Rescuing and Restructuring Firms in Difficulty* [2004] OJ C 244/2 (no longer in force).

- be unquoted immediately after the share issue;[35]
- have no more than £200,000 in gross assets immediately before the share issue;[36]
- have fewer than 25 full-time equivalent employees when the shares are issued;[37]
- not have received any investments under the Enterprise Investment Scheme or the Venture Capital Trusts scheme on or before the day the shares are issued;[38] and
- not have received more than £150,000 of SEIS investments, taking into account the current SEIS investment, other SEIS investments made on the same day, and any other SEIS investments made in the previous three years from the day before the shares are issued.[39]

Although both the SEIS and the ESI program require investee companies to be unlisted, the two schemes use different measures to determine whether a company is at an early stage of development. The SEIS looks at a company's gross assets and number of employees, whereas the ESI program focuses on its expenses and assessable income (see 4.2.1). Given that the VCLP and ESVCLP programs also use assets tests,[40] it is interesting that an assets test was not used under the ESI program. It is also worth noting that, unlike the SEIS, the ESI program does not contain any restrictions regarding a company receiving investments under its other venture capital tax incentive programs.

5.5.2 Ongoing Requirements

The ongoing requirements provide that the issuing company must meet the following conditions during certain time periods, referred to as 'Period A' and 'Period B'. Period A is the period beginning with the incorporation of a company and ending immediately before the third anniversary of the relevant share issue. Period B is the period beginning with the issue of the shares and ending immediately before the third anniversary of the issue.[41] The reference in both situations to the third anniversary of the share issue ties in with the minimum share holding period under the

---

[35] ITA 2007 (UK) s 257DF. An unquoted company means a company none of whose shares, stocks, debentures or other securities are marketed to the general public. A company's securities are taken to be marketed to the general public if they are listed on a recognised stock exchange.

[36] ITA 2007 (UK) s 257DI.

[37] ITA 2007 (UK) s 257DJ.

[38] ITA 2007 (UK) s 257DK.

[39] ITA 2007 (UK) s 257DL. Harper notes that unless a company has been 'preparing to trade' for a long period of time, this limit will effectively be a lifetime limit 'because after three years have passed they will no longer have a "new qualifying trade" for the purposes of the scheme': Harper, 'Finance Act Notes: Section 38 and Schedule 6: Seed Enterprise Investment Scheme' (n 9) 409.

[40] ITAA 1997 ss 118-425(6), 118-427(7), 118-440.

[41] ITA 2007 (UK) s 257 AC.

SEIS, which is three years (see 5.6). The requirements that a company must meet are as follows:

- During Period B, the company must exist wholly for the purpose of carrying on a 'new qualifying trade' (see below);[42]
- During Period B, the new qualifying trade, as well as any relevant preparation work and R&D,[43] must be carried on exclusively by the company itself, or by its qualifying 90% subsidiary;[44]
- During Period B, the company must have a permanent establishment in the United Kingdom;[45]
- During Period A, the company must not control any company which is not its 'qualifying subsidiary',[46] and the company generally must not be under the control of any other company (and no arrangements to contravene these requirements at any future point may exist);[47]
- During Period A, neither the company nor its qualifying 90% subsidiary may be a member of a partnership;[48]
- During Period B, any subsidiary that the company has must be a qualifying subsidiary;[49] and
- During Period B, any property managing subsidiary that the company has must be a qualifying 90% subsidiary of the company.[50]

---

[42] ITA 2007 (UK) s 257DA.

[43] Relevant preparation work refers to the activity of preparing to carry on a new qualifying trade which is intended (and has begun) to be carried on by the company or its qualifying 90% subsidiary. Preparations must be the subject of the company's relevant qualifying business activity. Relevant R&D refers to R&D which, immediately after the date the relevant shares are issued, the company or its qualifying 90% subsidiary carries on (or will begin to carry on), from which it is intended that a new qualifying trade will be derived, or will benefit. The R&D must be the subject of the company's relevant qualifying business activity: ITA 2007 (UK) ss 257 DC, 257HG.

[44] ITA 2007 (UK) ss 257 DC, 257HF.

[45] ITA 2007 (UK) s 257DD.

[46] A subsidiary is a qualifying subsidiary of another company ('the relevant company') for the purposes of the SEIS where: the subsidiary is a 51% subsidiary of the relevant company; no person other than the relevant company, or another of its subsidiaries, has control of the subsidiary; and no arrangements exist by virtue of which either of the above conditions would cease to be met: ITA 2007 (UK) ss 191, 257HJ.

[47] ITA 2007 (UK) s 257DG. It has been noted that the independence requirement is 'intended to prevent established trading companies from temporarily spinning off subsidiaries to allow investors access to the generous tax reliefs on offer': *United Kingdom, Parliamentary Debates, House of Commons, 11 June 2013, sitting 13, col 418 (David Gauke).*

[48] ITA 2007 (UK) s 257DH.

[49] ITA 2007 (UK) s 257DM.

[50] ITA 2007 (UK) s 257DN. A 'property managing subsidiary' means a subsidiary of the company whose business consists wholly or mainly in the holding or managing of land or any property deriving its value from land.

In relation to the first criterion, a qualifying trade will be 'new' where it has been carried on for two years or less on the day before the share issue.[51] This effectively imposes an age limit on companies under the SEIS and is consistent with the approach adopted under ESI program, which has its own age limits under the incorporation criterion of the early stage requirements (see 4.2.1). A qualifying trade is a business that is conducted on a commercial basis with a view to the realisation of profits that does not consist wholly or substantially of carrying on 'excluded activities' at any time during Period B.[52] Excluded activities include property development, dealing in land and securities, banking, money-lending, debt-factoring, hire-purchase financing or other financial activities, insurance, leasing activities and receiving royalties or licence fees.[53] Many of the excluded activities under the SEIS are similar to the 'ineligible activities' under the VCLP and ESVCLP programs (see 3.4). This indicates that the Australian and United Kingdom Governments share similar views on the types of activities that they do not wish to support under their respective programs. As noted at 4.2.2.2, no excluded activities have yet been prescribed under the ESI program, although it could be argued that the rigorous ESIC innovation requirements essentially remove the need for the Government to prescribe particular exclusions.

5.5.3 Absence of Specific Innovation Requirements

Unlike the ESI program, the SEIS does not include any specific innovation requirements that must be met by an investee company. By eschewing such requirements, the SEIS avoids some of the difficult issues that face the ESI program. However, it also means that the SEIS could provide tax relief for investments in early stage small businesses that may not necessarily be innovative. While this is a fundamental difference between the SEIS and the ESI program, it is interesting to note that the VCLP and ESVCLP programs, like the SEIS, also do not prescribe any specific innovation requirements for investee companies. The VCLP and ESVLP programs and the SEIS therefore operate in a similar way for the purposes of determining whether an investee company meets the relevant eligibility criteria – they focus on whether a company is engaged in ineligible or excluded activities rather than

[51] ITA 2007 (UK) ss 257 DC, 257HF.

[52] ITA 2007 (UK) ss 189, 257HF.

[53] Other excluded activities include: dealing in commodities, futures, shares or other financial instruments; dealing in goods otherwise than in the course of an ordinary trade of wholesale or retail distribution; providing legal or accountancy services; farming or market gardening; forestry activities or timber production; shipbuilding; producing coal or steel; operating or managing hotels; operating or managing nursing homes; generating or exporting electricity; generating heat or any other form of energy; and producing gas or fuel: see further ITA 2007 (UK) ss 192-199.

whether or not it meets prescribed innovation criteria as required under the ESI program.

5.6 Income Tax Relief

Unlike the ESI program, entitlement to tax relief under the SEIS does not arise automatically following the making of an eligible investment. Instead, under the SEIS, an investor is only entitled to make a claim for tax relief in relation to an amount subscribed for shares if they have received a 'compliance certificate' from the issuing company.[54] Before issuing a compliance certificate in respect of the relevant shares, the company must provide HM Revenue and Customs ('HMRC') with a compliance statement.[55] A compliance certificate may then be issued by the investee company on the authorisation of HMRC, stating that, except for the requirements that must be met by or in relation to the investor, the requirements for SEIS relief are met (for the time being) in relation to the shares issued to the investor.[56] A company cannot apply for a compliance certificate until it has been trading for at least four months, or it has spent at least 70% of the capital raised through the relevant share issue.[57] There is no upper time limit stipulating when a company must apply for a compliance certificate. The compliance certificate mechanism means that the SEIS is quite different to the ESI program, which uses a self-assessment system. In this regard, the process for obtaining tax relief under the SEIS is more cumbersome than the process under the ESI program. It should, nevertheless, be noted that ESI program has its own 'back-end reporting regime', which requires a company to provide information about shares it has issued during a financial year that could give rise to tax incentives under Subdivision 360-A of the ITAA 1997 (see 4.5).

Investors under the SEIS receive tax relief of 50% of the cost of purchasing shares in a qualifying company, up to a maximum annual investment of £100,000 (resulting in a maximum annual tax reduction of £50,000).[58] This can be compared with the 20% tax offset available under the ESI program, which is capped at $200,000 per year. The SEIS requires shares purchased by an investor to be held for a period of at least three years from the date of issue otherwise the relief is reduced or withdrawn.[59] This is very different from the ESI program, which does not pre-

[54] ITA 2007 (UK) s 257 EB.

[55] ITA 2007 (UK) s 257ED.

[56] ITA 2007 (UK) s 257EC.

[57] ITA 2007 (UK) s 257ED; HM Revenue & Customs, 'Venture Capital Schemes: SEIS: Income Tax Relief: Company and Investor Procedures: Company Procedures: Overview (HMRC Internal Manual, 16 October 2018) <https://www.gov.uk/hmrc-internal-manuals/venture-capital-schemes-manual/vcm35080>.

[58] ITA 2007 (UK) s 257AB.

[59] ITA 2007 (UK) s 257FA, FB.

scribe any minimum holding period for shares. Relief is also reduced or withdrawn if, during the three years from the date of issue of the shares:

- the investor becomes employed by the company without being a director of the company;[60]
- the investor's holding in the company becomes a 'substantial interest' (see 5.3);[61]
- the shares cease to be eligible shares, or there is a put or call option over them;[62]
- the company ceases to meet the qualifying conditions;[63]
- the company fails to spend the money raised by the share issue;[64] or
- the investor or associate receives 'value' from the company or from a person connected with that company.[65]

It is interesting to note that the operation of these ongoing requirements means that an action (or inaction) of the company can influence an investor's tax relief.

Tax relief under the SEIS cannot be carried forward, but it can be carried back to the previous income year by treating the shares as having been acquired in that year.[66] This is obviously quite different to the ESI program, where any excess tax offset may be carried forward indefinitely, but cannot be carried back.

Example
James invests £40,000 in qualifying SEIS shares in 2018–19. The SEIS income tax relief available is £20,000 (£40,000 × 50%). James has a £35,000 income tax liability for the year. He can reduce this liability to £15,000 (£35,000 – £20,000) as a result of his SEIS investment.

5.7 CGT Relief

Investors that receive tax relief under the SEIS in relation to shares in a qualifying company will generally be exempt from CGT on chargeable gains arising from the disposal of those shares, provided they hold the shares for at least three years.[67] However, if an investor invests more than £100,000 in SEIS shares, only a portion

[60] ITA 2007 (UK) ss 257BA, 257FR.

[61] ITA 2007 (UK) ss 257BB, 257FR.

[62] ITA 2007 (UK) ss 257CA, 257FC, 257FD.

[63] ITA 2007 (UK) ss 257DA-257DN, 257FR.

[64] ITA 2007 (UK) ss 257CC, 257FR.

[65] ITA 2007 (UK) ss 257FE-257FO; HM Revenue & Customs, 'Venture Capital Schemes Manual: SEIS: Income Tax Relief: Withdrawal or Reduction of SEIS Relief: Overview' (HMRC Internal Manual, 16 October 2018) <https://www.gov.uk/hmrc-internal-manuals/venture-capital-schemes-manual/vcm36010>. See ITA 2007 (UK) s 257FE as to the definition of value.

[66] ITA 2007 (UK) s 257AB.

[67] *Taxation of Chargeable Gains Act 1992* (UK) s 150E.

of the chargeable gain that arises on the sale of those shares will be exempt from CGT.[68] This portion is calculated as the amount of the chargeable gain multiplied by R/T, where R is the amount of income tax relief actually obtained, and T is the amount of the share subscription multiplied by 50%.

Example
In 2018–19, Jane subscribes £300,000 for 100,000 shares in a SEIS company. The maximum investment amount on which Jane can receive income tax relief in that year is £100,000. Jane sells all the shares in 2022–23 for £390,000, giving rise to a chargeable gain of £90,000.

The amount of income tax relief that Jane actually obtained (R) is £50,000, while the amount of the share subscription multiplied by 50% (T) is £150,000. Thus, only 1/3 (£50,000/£150,000) of Jane's gain is exempt from CGT: £90,000 × 1/3 = £30,000. Jane will be subject to CGT on the remaining 2/3 of her gain, which is £60,000.

The approach adopted under the SEIS is significantly different to the approach adopted under ESI program, where the tax offset cap of $200,000 does not limit the modified CGT treatment available in relation to ESIC shares. The limiting of the CGT relief under the SEIS helps to keep the costs of the scheme down, as it prevents investors from claiming unlimited CGT exemptions. This is particularly important because, as discussed below at 5.8, the SEIS also provides loss relief to investors, which adds to the cost of the scheme. In addition, the SEIS does not place an upper time limit on its CGT relief; the shares continue to be exempt from CGT regardless of how long they are held. This contrasts with the ESI program, which places a 10 year time limit on its CGT exemptions (see 4.4).

It should be noted that where a SEIS investor's income tax relief is reduced or withdrawn, the CGT exemption may also be correspondingly restricted.[69] Furthermore, if an investor is unable to claim income tax relief (e.g., because their income is too low or they have already reduced their income tax liability to nil through other reliefs), then their SEIS shares will also not be exempt from CGT.[70]

---

[68] *Taxation of Chargeable Gains Act 1992* (UK) s 150E(4), (5); HM Revenue & Customs, 'Venture Capital Schemes Manual: Seed Enterprise Investment Scheme (SEIS): SEIS Disposal Relief: Income Tax Relief Restricted' (HMRC Internal Manual, 16 October 2018) <https://www.gov.uk/hmrc-internal-manuals/venture-capital-schemes-manual/vcm40040>.

[69] HM Revenue & Customs, 'Venture Capital Schemes Manual: Seed Enterprise Investment Scheme (SEIS): SEIS Disposal Relief: CGT Exemption Restricted' (HMRC Internal Manual, 16 October 2018) <https://www.gov.uk/hmrc-internal-manuals/venture-capital-schemes-manual/vcm40030>.

[70] HM Revenue & Customs, 'Venture Capital Schemes Manual: Seed Enterprise Investment Scheme (SEIS): SEIS Disposal Relief: CGT Exemption' (HMRC Internal Manual, 16 October 2018) <https://www.gov.uk/hmrc-internal-manuals/venture-capital-schemes-manual/vcm40020>. However, this restriction does not apply if the investor's income tax liability is reduced to nil

In other words, they will miss out on CGT relief as a consequence of missing out on income tax relief.

5.8 Loss Relief

The SEIS does not prevent investors from claiming losses incurred on the disposal of their investments like the ESI program does. This is an attractive feature of the SEIS when compared with the ESI program. It is important to note that in working out whether a loss has been incurred for the purposes of claiming loss relief, the amount of any SEIS income tax relief that the investor has received in relation to their shares is taken into account. Where a loss would otherwise be made on the disposal of SEIS shares, the consideration paid for the shares is reduced by the amount of any SEIS tax relief that is attributable to them.[71] Any loss for the purposes of the SEIS is then calculated on the basis of this notionally reduced share purchase price. This is a fair approach as it takes into account the fact that the investor has previously received tax relief in relation to the shares. Allowing SEIS investors to claim losses (after taking into account any reduction for income tax relief) ensures that they are not penalised for making failed investments and are therefore in a similar position to ordinary non-SEIS investors who can claim their investment losses. This is in marked contrast to the situation that exists under the ESI program (as well as the VCLP and ESVCLP programs), where losses cannot be claimed and investors are therefore effectively punished for making unsuccessful investments.

Example

Jenny pays £100,000 to subscribe for shares in a SEIS company in the 2018–19 income year. She receives income tax relief of £50,000 in that year. In the 2032–33 income year, Jenny sells all her shares for £40,000, giving rise to a £60,000 loss (£100,000 – £40,000 = £60,000).

However, in working out the loss that Jenny can actually claim, the £100,000 that she paid as consideration for her shares is reduced by the £50,000 of income tax relief that is attributable to the shares under the SEIS. This means that Jenny can claim a loss of only £10,000 (£50,000 – £40,000 = £10,000).

In contrast, if Jenny had instead sold the shares for £70,000 (resulting in a loss of £30,000), she would not be able to claim a loss under the SEIS because the notionally reduced purchase price (£50,000) would be less than the sale price (£70,000).

---

because of the SEIS income tax relief: HM Revenue & Customs, 'Venture Capital Schemes Manual: Seed Enterprise Investment Scheme (SEIS): SEIS Disposal Relief: Income Tax Relief Restricted' (n 68).

[71] *Taxation of Chargeable Gains Act 1992* (UK) s 150E.

5.9 Reinvestment Relief

The SEIS also provides investors with a special kind of incentive known as reinvestment relief.[72] This relief is available where an individual disposes of any asset that gives rise to a chargeable gain (the 'original disposal'), and they reinvest all or part of that gain in shares that qualify for SEIS relief (up to £100,000).[73] In these circumstances, half of the reinvestment amount may be exempt from CGT in regard to the original disposal (up to £50,000).[74] Reinvestment relief is likely to provide a strong inducement for investors who have chargeable gains to make SEIS investments in order to minimise their tax liability. Interestingly, the original disposal does not actually have to be made before the relevant SEIS shares are issued. A chargeable gain for which an investor claims reinvestment relief may arise after the issue of SEIS shares, provided that the investor still holds those shares.[75]

Example
In the 2018–19 income year, John disposes of property which gives rise to a chargeable gain of £100,000. He uses money from the property sale to subscribe for £80,000 of shares in a SEIS company.

John claims the full amount of SEIS income tax relief in respect of the share issue (£40,000). John also claims reinvestment relief in respect of the share issue. Half of John's £80,000 investment amount can be set off against the £100,000 gain made on the disposal of his property. Therefore, the chargeable gain that John makes on the disposal of his property is reduced to £60,000 (£100,000– £40,000).

---

[72] Reinvestment relief was originally meant to be a temporary measure, but was extended in 2014. It was originally introduced 'to kick-start the scheme and create a buzz': *United Kingdom, Parliamentary Debates, House of Commons, 11 June 2013, sitting 13, col 418 (David Gauke)*. The relief was extended as a response to a perceived slow take up of the SEIS. One commentator has, however, questioned whether this was an appropriate response, considering that the scheme was 'already one of the most generous investment incentives of its kind': Harper, 'Finance Act Notes: Section 56: SEIS: Income Tax Relief; Section 57: SEIS: Re-Investment Relief' (n 19) 445.

[73] HM Revenue & Customs, 'HS393 Seed Enterprise Investment Scheme – Income Tax and Capital Gains Tax reliefs (2018)' (Guidance, 9 April 2018) <https://www.gov.uk/government/publications/seed-enterprise-investment-scheme-income-tax-and-capital-gains-tax-reliefs-hs393-self-assessment-helpsheet/hs393-seed-enterprise-investment-scheme-income-tax-and-capital-gains-tax-reliefs-2018#which-seis-shares-qualify-for-reinvestment-relief>.

[74] *Taxation of Chargeable Gains Act 1992* (UK) s 150G, Sch 5BB. See further HM Revenue & Customs, 'Venture Capital Schemes Manual: Seed Enterprise Investment Scheme (SEIS): Re-Investment Relief: Introduction' (HMRC Internal Manual, 16 October 2018) <https://www.gov.uk/hmrc-internal-manuals/venture-capital-schemes-manual/vcm45010>.

[75] HM Revenue & Customs, 'HS393 Seed Enterprise Investment Scheme – Income Tax and Capital Gains Tax reliefs (2018)' (n 73).

In order to benefit from reinvestment relief, investors must receive SEIS income tax relief in respect of the reinvested amount. If the income tax relief is withdrawn or reduced, for instance because the ongoing SEIS company requirements cease to be met during the required time period, there is a corresponding withdrawal or reduction of reinvestment relief.[76] Reinvestment relief may also be restricted where income tax relief is not given on the full amount of a share subscription.[77]

5.10 Conclusion

This chapter has closely examined the SEIS and compared and contrasted it with the ESI program as well as the VCLP and ESVCLP programs. As was noted in Chap. 1, the SEIS was rated by the European Commission in 2017 as the best angel tax incentive across 36 sample countries in terms of good practice.[78] There were certain design aspects of the SEIS that drove its high rating. These included the provision of loss relief (which helps de-risk investments),[79] the use of a combination of age, size and excluded sectors to target entrepreneurial firms (in order to mitigate the problems associated with 'picking winners'),[80] the focus on newly issued ordinary shares, and the special provision for angel investors to participate in the management of their investee companies.[81] From a regulatory perspective, the European Commission appreciated that the SEIS caps the maximum tax relief available to investors in order to keep the scheme affordable, imposes a minimum holding period for shares, and administers the scheme on a non-discretionary basis with transparent annual cost monitoring.[82] While some of these positive features are also incorporated in the ESI program, it is clear that the ESI program is quite deliberately designed to be different in many respects from the SEIS. There are, nevertheless, certain additional features of the SEIS that could have been incorporated in the ESI program to improve its policy outcomes. We consider some of these features in the final chapter of this book, in which we make a number of suggestions for reforming the ESI program in order to improve its policy outcomes.

---

[76] HM Revenue & Customs, 'Venture Capital Schemes Manual: Seed Enterprise Investment Scheme (SEIS): Re-Investment Relief: Relief Reduced or Withdrawn' (HMRC Internal Manual, 16 October 2018) <https://www.gov.uk/hmrc-internal-manuals/venture-capital-schemes-manual/vcm45090>.

[77] HM Revenue & Customs, 'Venture Capital Schemes Manual: Seed Enterprise Investment Scheme (SEIS): Re-investment Relief: Relief Restricted' (16 October 2018) <https://www.gov.uk/hmrc-internal-manuals/venture-capital-schemes-manual/vcm45040>.

[78] These countries comprised the European Union nations as well as selected OECD countries: European Commission (n 18) 4, 202.

[79] The European Commission has noted that the provision of loss relief has been linked with encouraging greater risk-taking among investors: ibid 11.

[80] Ibid 204.

[81] Ibid 202–3.

[82] Ibid.

References

Community Guidelines on State Aid for Rescuing and Restructuring Firms in Difficulty [2004] OJ C 244/2

European Commission, 'Effectiveness of Tax Incentives for Venture Capital and Business Angels to Foster the Investment of SMEs and Start-ups: Final Report' (Working Paper No 68, European Commission, June 2017)

Explanatory Memorandum, Tax Laws Amendment (Tax Incentives for Innovation) Bill 2016 (Cth)

Finance Act 2012 (UK)

Harper, Andrew, 'Finance Act Notes: Section 38 and Schedule 6: Seed Enterprise Investment Scheme' (2012) 4 *British Tax Review* 407

Harper, Andrew, 'Finance Act Notes: Section 56: SEIS: Income Tax Relief; Section 57: SEIS: Re-Investment Relief' (2013) 4 *British Tax Review* 443

HM Revenue & Customs, 'Apply for Advance Assurance on a Venture Capital Scheme' (Guidance, 31 August 2018) <https://www.gov.uk/guidance/venture-capital-schemes-apply-for-advance-assurance>

HM Revenue & Customs, 'Enterprise Investment Scheme and Seed Enterprise Investment Scheme' (Statistics, April 2017) <https://www.gov.uk/government/uploads/system/uploads/attachment_data/file/611525/Combined_tables_to_publish.pdf>

HM Revenue & Customs, 'Enterprise Investment Scheme and Seed Enterprise Investment Scheme April 2017 Statistics on Companies Raising Funds' (Official Statistics Release, 27 April 2017) <https://www.gov.uk/government/uploads/system/uploads/attachment_data/file/611524/April_2017_Commentary_EIS_SEIS_Official_Statistics_v5.pdf>

HM Revenue & Customs, 'HS393 Seed Enterprise Investment Scheme – Income Tax and Capital Gains Tax reliefs (2018)' (Guidance, 9 April 2018) <https://www.gov.uk/government/publications/seed-enterprise-investment-scheme-income-tax-and-capital-gains-tax-reliefs-hs393-self-assessment-helpsheet/hs393-seed-enterprise-investment-scheme-income-tax-and-capital-gains-tax-reliefs-2018#which-seis-shares-qualify-for-reinvestment-relief>

HM Revenue & Customs, 'Income Tax: Venture Capital Schemes – Risk to Capital Condition' (Policy Paper, 22 November 2017) <https://www.gov.uk/government/publications/income-tax-venture-capital-schemes-risk-to-capital-condition/income-tax-venture-capital-schemes-risk-to-capital-condition>

HM Revenue & Customs, 'Tax Relief for Investors Using Venture Capital Schemes' (Guidance, 3 October 2018) <https://www.gov.uk/guidance/venture-capital-schemes-tax-relief-for-investors>

HM Revenue & Customs, 'Use the Enterprise Investment Scheme (EIS) to Raise Money for Your Company' (Guidance, 12 October 2018) <https://www.gov.uk/guidance/venture-capital-schemes-apply-for-the-enterprise-investment-scheme>

HM Revenue & Customs, 'Venture Capital Schemes Manual: EIS: Income Tax Relief: Supplementary and General: Approved Investment Fund as Nominee' (HMRC Internal Manual, 16 October 2018) <https://www.gov.uk/hmrc-internal-manuals/venture-capital-schemes-manual/vcm16050>

HM Revenue & Customs, 'Venture Capital Schemes Manual: Risk-To-Capital Condition: An Overview of the Risk-To-Capital Condition' (HMRC Internal Manual, 16 October 2018) <https://www.gov.uk/hmrc-internal-manuals/venture-capital-schemes-manual/vcm8530>

HM Revenue & Customs, 'Venture Capital Schemes Manual: Seed Enterprise Investment Scheme (SEIS): Re-Investment Relief: Introduction' (HMRC Internal Manual, 16 October 2018) <https://www.gov.uk/hmrc-internal-manuals/venture-capital-schemes-manual/vcm45010>

HM Revenue & Customs, 'Venture Capital Schemes Manual: Seed Enterprise Investment Scheme (SEIS): Re-Investment Relief: Relief Reduced or Withdrawn' (HMRC Internal Manual, 16 October 2018) <https://www.gov.uk/hmrc-internal-manuals/venture-capital-schemes-manual/vcm45090>

HM Revenue & Customs, 'Venture Capital Schemes Manual: Seed Enterprise Investment Scheme (SEIS): Re-investment Relief: Relief Restricted' (16 October 2018) <https://www.gov.uk/hmrc-internal-manuals/venture-capital-schemes-manual/vcm45040>

HM Revenue & Customs, 'Venture Capital Schemes Manual: Seed Enterprise Investment Scheme (SEIS): SEIS Disposal Relief: CGT Exemption' (HMRC Internal Manual, 16 October 2018) <https://www.gov.uk/hmrc-internal-manuals/venture-capital-schemes-manual/vcm40020>

HM Revenue & Customs, 'Venture Capital Schemes Manual: Seed Enterprise Investment Scheme (SEIS): SEIS Disposal Relief: Income Tax Relief Restricted' (HMRC Internal Manual, 16 October 2018) <https://www.gov.uk/hmrc-internal-manuals/venture-capital-schemes-manual/vcm40040>

HM Revenue & Customs, 'Venture Capital Schemes Manual: Seed Enterprise Investment Scheme (SEIS): SEIS Disposal Relief: CGT Exemption Restricted' (HMRC Internal Manual, 16 October 2018) <https://www.gov.uk/hmrc-internal-manuals/venture-capital-schemes-manual/vcm40030>

HM Revenue & Customs, 'Venture Capital Schemes Manual: SEIS: Income Tax Relief: General Requirements: No Disqualifying Arrangements Requirement' (HMRC Internal Manual, 16 October 2018) <https://www.gov.uk/hmrc-internal-manuals/venture-capital-schemes-manual/vcm33080>

HM Revenue & Customs, 'Venture Capital Schemes Manual: SEIS: Income Tax Relief: Supplementary and General: Nominees and Bare Trustees' (HMRC Internal Manual, 16 October 2018) <https://www.gov.uk/hmrc-internal-manuals/venture-capital-schemes-manual/vcm37040>

HM Revenue & Customs, 'Venture Capital Schemes Manual: SEIS: Income Tax Relief: The Investor: No Employee Investors' (HMRC Internal Manual, 16 October 2018) <https://www.gov.uk/hmrc-internal-manuals/venture-capital-schemes-manual/vcm32020>

HM Revenue & Customs, 'Venture Capital Schemes Manual: SEIS: Income Tax Relief: Withdrawal or Reduction of SEIS Relief: Overview' (HMRC Internal Manual, 16 October 2018) <https://www.gov.uk/hmrc-internal-manuals/venture-capital-schemes-manual/vcm36010>

HM Revenue & Customs, 'Venture Capital Schemes: SEIS: Income Tax Relief: Company and Investor Procedures: Company Procedures: Overview (HMRC Internal Manual, 16 October 2018) <https://www.gov.uk/hmrc-internal-manuals/venture-capital-schemes-manual/vcm35080>

HM Revenue & Customs, 'Venture Capital Schemes Manual: Venture Capital Trusts: Contents' (HMRC Internal Manual, 16 October 2018) <https://www.gov.uk/hmrc-internal-manuals/venture-capital-schemes-manual/vcm50000>

Income Tax Act 2007 (UK)

Income Tax Assessment Act 1936 (Cth)

Income Tax Assessment Act 1997 (Cth)

Taxation of Chargeable Gains Act 1992 (UK)

United Kingdom, Parliamentary Debates, House of Commons, 11 June 2013, sitting 13, col 418 (David Gauke)

Chapter 6
Suggestions for Reforming Australia's Early Stage Investor Program

Abstract This book has examined the critical role that venture capital investment plays in supporting start-ups and the importance of these companies' success for the development of a country's innovation system. The earlier chapters focused on a number of tax incentive programs that have been introduced by the Australian and United Kingdom Governments to encourage venture capital investment. In particular, Chap. 3 examined Australia's formal venture capital tax incentive programs, Chap. 4 examined Australia's new ESI program and Chap. 5 examined the United Kingdom's SEIS (on which the ESI program was loosely modelled). Building on the policy framework and detailed discussion set out in these earlier chapters, this chapter makes some suggestions for reforming the ESI program so that it might be able to better achieve its policy objectives. The suggestions draw on comparisons made between the ESI program and the SEIS, as well as aspects of Australia's formal venture capital tax incentive programs. The reform options put forward in this chapter involve: providing ISA with the power to make rulings in determining whether a company qualifies as an ESIC; allowing investors to claim capital losses on the disposal of their ESIC shares; introducing reinvestment relief similar to that provided under the SEIS; extending an angel tax incentive to investment in later stage companies to ensure that companies are supported throughout their stages of growth; and removing the 10 year CGT limit. The chapter concludes by recognising the importance of the ESI program to Australia's innovation system and its critical role in helping Australia remain a clever country in the twenty-first century.

6.1 Introduction

It is clear from the discussion in the previous chapters of this book that although Australia's ESI program was loosely modelled on the United Kingdom's SEIS, it has several unique features that make it quite a distinct venture capital tax incentive program in its own right. While both the ESI program and the SEIS clearly share the same broad policy objective of stimulating angel investment in their countries' start-ups, they have different eligibility requirements and provide different tax incentives.

S. Barkoczy, T. Wilkinson, *Incentivising Angels*, SpringerBriefs in Law,
https://doi.org/10.1007/978-981-13-6632-1_6

The ESI program has a number of positive features, which are, arguably, improvements on the SEIS. One of these is that, unlike the SEIS, the ESI program assesses companies only against point-in-time requirements (rather than both point-in-time and ongoing requirements), which simplifies the program and increases certainty for companies and investors. Another positive feature is that the ESI program uses tailored but flexible innovation tests to ensure that it targets only those early stage companies that are truly innovative and engaged in commercialising new or significantly improved products, processes and services. Nevertheless, there are also aspects of the ESI program that could arguably be improved. This final chapter draws on the discussion of Australia's formal venture capital tax incentive programs in Chap. 3 and the United Kingdom's SEIS in Chap. 5 to make some suggestions for ways that the ESI program might possibly be reformed to better achieve its policy objectives.

6.2 Providing Innovation and Science Australia with the Power to Make Rulings

As discussed at 4.2, the concept of an ESIC is a fundamental cornerstone of the ESI program. It will be recalled that whether a company qualifies as an ESIC depends on whether it satisfies a set of early stage (see 4.2.1) and innovation (see 4.2.2) requirements. However, as the discussion at 4.2.3 indicates, the process of determining whether a company meets these requirements is not necessarily straightforward. While the early stage requirements are likely to be relatively easy for companies to self-assess, the innovation requirements may be more challenging, and in many cases there is likely to be some uncertainty as to whether they have been met. This is particularly the case in relation to the application of the principles-based innovation test, which uses subjective language and nebulous criteria.

As mentioned at 4.2.4, the Commissioner of Taxation can make both private and public rulings in relation to determining whether a company satisfies the ESIC requirements. Because the risk of incorrectly claiming the ESI tax incentive lies with investors, many investors may be justifiably wary of making an investment without first obtaining the certainty of a tax ruling.[1] However, there are practical concerns in using the current taxation ruling system for the purpose of determining whether a company qualifies as an ESIC. The major concern is that an investor will not technically be protected by a ruling that is issued to the company as the investor

[1] See Michael Bailey, 'Early Stage Innovation Company investor tax breaks misunderstood', *Australian Financial Review* (online), 4 May 2017 <http://www.afr.com/leadership/entrepreneur/early-stage-innovation-company-investor-tax-breaks-misunderstood-by-founders-investors-20170504-gvyr4x#ixzz4idVpA5H7> and Carlos Gouveia, *Early Stage Innovation Companies – 10 Months On* (27 April 2017) Colin Biggers & Paisley Lawyers <https://www.cbp.com.au/insights/2017/april/early-stage-innovation-companies-10-months-on>.

is not the applicant. Another issue that arises is that a company's ESIC status will not be protected by the ruling if the company's circumstances change in the meantime.

It is therefore suggested that a special rulings regime addressing these concerns should be introduced, and that the body responsible for making such rulings should be ISA (rather than the ATO), due to its particular innovation expertise.[2] ISA already has important responsibilities and plays a key role as a dual regulator with the ATO in relation to the R&D tax incentive[3] and the VCLP and ESVCLP programs.[4] In particular, in relation to the VCLP and ESVCLP programs, it has a special power to make binding public and private rulings on whether activities are 'not ineligible activities' under these programs (see 3.4), as well as a power to make public and private findings on whether activities within a specified class are a substantially novel application of one or more technologies.[5] Given the uncertainties facing investors and companies under the ESI program, it is suggested that similar powers should be granted to ISA for the purpose of ruling on whether a company qualifies as an ESIC and ensuring that its rulings protect investors even though they may be applied for by their investee companies. This reform would free up the ATO to deal with technical tax matters and ensure that rulings on the ESIC status of a company are made by the agency with the most appropriate specialist skills in assessing innovation criteria.

6.3 Allowing Capital Losses

The treatment of capital losses under the ESI program is one of the biggest points of difference between the ESI program and the SEIS. While investors under the ESI program must disregard their losses (see 4.4), investors under the SEIS are permitted to claim their losses (see 5.8). It is acknowledged that the requirement for

---

[2] One commentator has observed that ISA already plays a role in providing guidance to the ATO in relation to the ESI program: see Dragan Misic, 'New Approach to Capital Raising: Tax Perspective' (2017) 21(2) *The Tax Specialist* 65, 67. It is interesting to note that the ATO states on its website that when issuing rulings relating to the principles-based innovation test it may, in any case, need to consult with the Department of Industry, Innovation and Science: Australian Taxation Office, *Principles-based Innovation Test* (2 August 2017) <https://www.ato.gov.au/Business/Tax-incentives-for-innovation/In-detail/Tax-incentives-for-early-stage-investors/?page=3#Principles_based_innovation_test>.

[3] ISA is required to register R&D entities in respect of their R&D activities and is empowered to make findings on certain innovation-related matters under the *Industry Research and Development Act 1986* (Cth).

[4] ISA is responsible for registering and regulating VCLPs and ESVCLPs and making certain determinations in relation to investment requirements: TAA Division 362; *Venture Capital Act 2002* (Cth) Division 25 of Part 4.

[5] The latter power was granted in 2018 in order to increase certainty about the status of investments under the VCLP and ESVCLP programs: Explanatory Memorandum, Treasury Laws Amendment (Tax Integrity and Other Measures) Bill 2018 (Cth) 3.15.

investors to disregard their losses on ESIC investments is designed to provide symmetry with the way in which the ESI program treats their gains. It also ensures that gains and losses under the ESI program are treated consistently with the way that gains and losses are treated under the VCLP and ESVCLP programs. Nevertheless, it is submitted that it would be much fairer to allow investors to claim losses on their ESIC investments, as this would put them in the same position as investors who make losses on shares in other companies and who are not required to disregard such losses. Currently, investors who take risks and make unsuccessful investments in ESICs are actually treated punitively under the ESI program compared with other investors. This is contrary to the underlying rationale of a tax incentive. The situation is compounded by the fact that, due to the very early stage at which ESIC investments are made, investors in these companies are likely to encounter losses more frequently than other investors.

It is submitted that the United Kingdom's SEIS uses a sensible method for calculating losses that would be appropriate to adopt under the ESI program. As discussed at 5.8, this approach takes into account the front-end tax benefit that an investor has received in the calculation of the amount of their loss. It will be recalled that under the SEIS, where an investor makes a loss on the disposal of their SEIS shares, the consideration paid for the shares is reduced by the amount of any SEIS tax relief that is attributable to those shares. Any loss is then calculated on the basis of the reduced share purchase price. This seems to be a fair approach as it takes into account the fact that the investor has previously received tax relief in relation to the shares. Adopting a similar approach under the ESI program would ensure that ESIC investors are not prejudiced in the treatment of their losses when compared with other investors. This would essentially place them in the same position that they would be in if they had made an investment in any other company.

It is acknowledged that allowing investors to claim losses is likely to significantly add to the cost of the ESI program. The failure rate of early stage companies is already high, and there is some overseas evidence which suggests that providing investors with loss relief encourages risky investment in young, growing and innovative businesses by addressing investor risk aversion.[6] This means that where governments provide loss relief, more losses might actually end up arising because more risky investments are being made. Nevertheless, this reform would promote equity between different kinds of investors, and it is likely that it would also help encourage uptake of the ESI program.[7]

---

[6] European Commission, 'Effectiveness of Tax Incentives for Venture Capital and Business Angels to Foster the Investment of SMEs and Start-ups: Final Report' (Working Paper No 68, European Commission, June 2017) 11.

[7] It is worth noting that some stakeholders (particularly venture capital funds) have also called for losses to be allowed under the ESVCLP program, suggesting that allowing losses would increase the uptake of the program and avoid punishing investors who make failed investments: see, e.g., submissions from venture capital funds Brandon Capital Partners and OneVentures in Australian Government, The Board of Taxation, *Review of Taxation Arrangements under the Venture Capital Limited Partnership Regime: A Report to the Assistant Treasurer* (Report, June 2011) 37. However, the Government has remained steadfast in its opposition to this. The Board of Taxation has stated

6.4 Introducing Reinvestment Relief

One of the features of the SEIS that the Australian Government chose not to replicate when designing the ESI program was the special reinvestment relief available to investors (see 5.9). It will be recalled that SEIS reinvestment relief applies where an individual disposes of an asset that gives rise to a chargeable gain, and they reinvest all or part of that gain in shares that qualify for SEIS tax relief (up to £100,000). Although this measure was originally introduced as a temporary measure to stimulate interest in the scheme,[8] SEIS reinvestment relief was extended indefinitely in 2014. It is submitted that the introduction of a similar kind of tax relief under the ESI program could increase uptake of the program and direct more capital to ESICs.

Introducing such an incentive would, however, expose the Government to additional costs in terms of foregone revenue. In addition, there is also a risk that it may lead to investments being made for the 'wrong' reasons (i.e., to minimise CGT, rather than to support worthy startups). This could be problematic, as entities that invest purely for tax reasons may take less care in the selection of their investments and may be less likely to take an active interest in their investees (which could lead to higher rates of failed investments). While these considerations are not insignificant, the Government may nevertheless wish to consider the option of introducing reinvestment relief under the ESI program at some point in the future, especially if data on the program indicates that there is low uptake. To avoid exposing itself to significant costs, the Government could cap the amount of capital gains that an investor can reinvest in an ESIC.

6.5 Extending the Incentive to Investment in Later Stage Companies

The ESI program's early stage requirements, especially the assessable income criterion, ensure that companies that have moved beyond the seed and pre-commercialisation phases, such as those that are in the early expansion and later stages of development, will not qualify as ESICs. The rationale for confining the incentive in this way is to ensure that funding is channelled towards those companies that are unlikely to get much support from Australia's formal venture capital tax incentive programs and are therefore most at risk of experiencing financing problems.

---

that it is 'difficult to see the rationale for a proposition whereby … investors could receive tax exempt gains and at the same time be entitled to deductions for losses'. It further noted that allowing losses would represent a significant cost to revenue, given that losses arise frequently under the ESVCLP program: at 38.

[8] United Kingdom, *Parliamentary Debates*, House of Commons, 11 June 2013, sitting 13, col. 418 (David Gauke).

In the United Kingdom, companies that outgrow the SEIS may be able to receive support under the Enterprise Investment Scheme before potentially moving on to the formal Venture Capital Trusts scheme. It is arguable that Australia may, in a sense, be missing the 'middle step' provided by the Enterprise Investment Scheme in the United Kingdom, as it has no similar informal incentive. Instead, companies that do not qualify as ESICs will generally have to rely on the VCLP and ESVCLP programs for investment. However, the reality is that many companies that just miss out on qualifying as ESICs may still be too underdeveloped to garner much interest from the formal venture capital market. In addition, even those companies that qualify as ESICs may struggle to access follow-on funding after their initial investment and this may significantly hamper their future development prospects. The Australian Government should carefully monitor the situation to ensure that companies are not also encountering another funding gap at a later stage. If this occurs, additional support may be warranted.

If the Government wishes to extend an angel tax incentive to investment in later stage companies, it will need to prescribe appropriate eligibility criteria and determine the kinds of incentives it is willing to provide. In this regard, it could take a similar approach to the United Kingdom's Enterprise Investment Scheme, where less-generous tax incentives are provided to investors in later stage companies. For example, one option could be to provide a lower rate of front-end tax incentive or to remove the front-end tax incentive altogether and only provide a back-end tax incentive for later stage investment. This would recognise that there is a lower risk of investing in companies that have passed the seed and pre-commercialisation phases.

6.6 Removing the 10 Year CGT Limit

Investors seeking to make venture capital investments in Australia need to determine whether they wish to invest indirectly in start-ups through venture capital funds or directly as angels. Different consequences, including different tax incentives, flow from this decision. Where investors wish to rely on the expertise of a fund manager to make investments, rather than engaging directly with a start-up themselves, they will be able to utilise the VCLP or ESVCLP programs. Investing through a fund relieves the investor of the need to select investments, perform due diligence, monitor investees and negotiate exits. Where investors wish to take a more hands-on approach, however, the ESI program may suit their needs and the tax incentives available under the program are likely to be very attractive. These tax incentives are intended to compensate angel investors for the more onerous and risky investments that they make in very early stage companies.

It is logical that, out of Australia's venture capital tax incentive programs, the ESI program provides the most generous tax incentives, followed by the ESVCLP program and then the VCLP program. It is interesting to note, however, that while the ESI program offers an upfront tax offset at the rate of 20% (double the 10% tax offset offered under the ESVCLP program), it provides less generous CGT exemptions than the VCLP and ESVCLP programs. The CGT exemptions under the ESI program only operate for 10 years, after which time capital gains are taxed (albeit on a modified basis). In contrast, the CGT exemptions under the ESVCLP and VCLP programs are not subject to any time limits. Although it is acknowledged that imposing a cap on CGT exemptions helps to control the cost of the program, the Government may wish to consider removing the 10 year limit on the CGT exemption under the ESI program in order to increase uptake in the program and standardise the treatment with Australia's formal venture capital tax incentive programs.

6.7 Conclusion

It has been argued that the nations that will have the most dynamic and vibrant economies in the twenty-first century are likely to be those that 'are best able to support the commercialisation of innovative discoveries, inventions and technologies developed by their start-up and early stage companies'.[9] This makes new initiatives such as the ESI program, which attempts to address a long-standing market failure in the provision of early stage finance to Australian start-ups, vitally important. While the ESI program comes at an immediate cost to the Government in terms of the revenue it collects, it stands to enhance Australia's innovation system, produce a range of spillover benefits to the broader economy, and help retain entrepreneurs in Australia. This, in turn, should help increase tax revenue for the Government in the long term.

The Australian Government has recognised that if Australia wants to remain a lucky country, it must nurture an environment in which innovation and entrepreneurship can thrive.[10] Having an active formal venture capital market is unquestionably crucial to achieving this goal. The Government has been supporting the formal venture capital sector for over 30 years through its MIC, PDF, VCLP and ESVCLP programs, and this has undoubtedly stimulated venture capital activity in Australia. It is, however, equally important for Australia to also have a vibrant network of angels that are actively investing in start-ups, especially those at the seed and pre-commercialisation stages where significant funding gaps are likely to exist. The Turnbull Government's decision to introduce the ESI program in 2016 is a welcome measure that demonstrates that Australia is now also committed to supporting this hitherto 'overlooked' group of investors.

Designing incentives to stimulate venture capital investment can be tricky, and there is no guarantee that the ESI program will necessarily be successful. Many countries have developed venture capital programs that have failed to deliver what

---

[9] Stephen Barkoczy, Tamara Wilkinson, Ann Monotti and Mark Davison, *Innovation and Venture Capital Law and Policy* (Federation Press, 2016) 33.

[10] See Australian Government, Department of Industry, Innovation and Science, Office of the Chief Economist, *Australian Industry Report 2015* (Report, 2015) 1.

they have promised. As Lerner has observed, 'for each effective government intervention, there have been dozens, even hundreds, of failures, where substantial public expenditures bore no fruit'.[11] He adds that, in many cases, these failures were entirely predictable as they were based on flawed designs.[12] According to Lerner, governments have 'squandered many billions of dollars on ill-conceived efforts' and have ironically sometimes 'even left their entrepreneurial sectors in worse shape than before'.[13] Nevertheless, as former Prime Minister Turnbull noted when he launched his Government's National Innovation and Science Agenda, which foreshadowed the introduction of the ESI program:

> We have got to be prepared to take risks. … [If] some of these policies are not as successful as we like, we will change them. We will learn from them. Because that is what a 21st century government has got to be. It has got to be as agile as the start-up businesses it seeks to inspire.[14]

References

Australian Government, Department of Industry, Innovation and Science, Office of the Chief Economist, *Australian Industry Report 2015* (Report, 2015)

Australian Government, the Board of Taxation, *Review of Taxation Arrangements under the Venture Capital Limited Partnership Regime: A Report to the Assistant Treasurer* (Report, June 2011)

Australian Taxation Office, *Principles-based Innovation Test* (2 August 2017) <https://www.ato.gov.au/Business/Tax-incentives-for-innovation/In-detail/Tax-incentives-for-early-stage-investors/?page=3#Principles_based_innovation_test>

Bailey, Michael, 'Early Stage Innovation Company Investor Tax Breaks Misunderstood', *Australian Financial Review* (online), 4 May 2017 <http://www.afr.com/leadership/entrepreneur/early-stage-innovation-company-investor-tax-breaks-misunderstood-by-founders-investors-20170504-gvyr4x#ixzz4idVpA5H7>

Barkoczy, Stephen, Tamara Wilkinson, Ann Monotti and Mark Davison, *Innovation and Venture Capital Law and Policy* (Federation Press, 2016)

European Commission, 'Effectiveness of Tax Incentives for Venture Capital and Business Angels to Foster the Investment of SMEs and Start-ups: Final Report' (Working Paper No 68, European Commission, June 2017)

Explanatory Memorandum, Treasury Laws Amendment (Tax Integrity and Other Measures) Bill 2018 (Cth)

Gouveia, Carlos, *Early Stage Innovation Companies – 10 Months On* (27 April 2017) Colin Biggers & Paisley Lawyers <https://www.cbp.com.au/insights/2017/april/early-stage-innovation-companies-10-months-on>

Industry Research and Development Act 1986 (Cth)

[11] Josh Lerner, *Boulevard of Broken Dreams: Why Public Efforts to Boost Entrepreneurship and Venture Capital Have Failed – and What to Do About It* (Princeton University Press, 2009) 5.

[12] Ibid.

[13] Ibid 89.

[14] Prime Minister and Minister for Industry, Innovation and Science, 'Launch of the National Innovation and Science Agenda' (Media Release, 7 December 2015) <http://www.pm.gov.au/media/2015-12-07/launch-national-innovation-and-science-agenda>.

Lerner, Josh, *Boulevard of Broken Dreams: Why Public Efforts to Boost Entrepreneurship and Venture Capital Have Failed – and What to Do About It* (Princeton University Press, 2009)

Misic, Dragan, 'New Approach to Capital Raising: Tax Perspective' (2017) 21(2) *The Tax Specialist* 65

Prime Minister and Minister for Industry, Innovation and Science, 'Launch of the National Innovation and Science Agenda' (Media Release, 7 December 2015) <http://www.pm.gov.au/media/2015-12-07/launch-national-innovation-and-science-agenda>

Tax Administration Act 1953 (Cth)

United Kingdom, *Parliamentary Debates*, House of Commons, 11 June 2013, sitting 13, col 418 (David Gauke)

Venture Capital Act 2002 (Cth)

Appendix: ESI Program Legislation[1]

Division 360—Early stage investors in innovation companies
Table of Subdivisions

Subdivision 360-A—Tax incentives for early stage investors in innovation companies
Guide to Subdivision 360-A

360-5 What This Subdivision is About

You may be entitled to a tax offset if you are, or a trust or partnership of which you are a member is, issued with certain kinds of equity interests in a small Australian company with high-growth potential that is engaging in innovative activities.

A modified CGT treatment may also apply to those equity interests.

Table of Sections

Operative provisions

[1] Sourced from the Federal Register of Legislation at 21 December 2018. For the latest information on Australian Government law please go to https://www.legislation.gov.au.

S. Barkoczy, T. Wilkinson, *Incentivising Angels*, SpringerBriefs in Law,
https://doi.org/10.1007/978-981-13-6632-1

Operative Provisions
360-10 Object of this Subdivision

The object of this Subdivision is to encourage new investment in small Australian innovation companies with high-growth potential by providing qualifying investors with a tax offset and a modified CGT treatment.

360-15 Entitlement to the tax offset

General case

(1) You are entitled to a *tax offset for an income year if:

(a) you are none of the following:

(i) a trust or a partnership;
(ii) a *widely held company or a *100% subsidiary of a widely held company; and

(b) at a particular time during the income year, a company issues you with *equity interests that are *shares in the company; and
(c) subsection 360-40(1) (about early stage innovation companies) applies to the company immediately after that time; and
(d) neither you nor the company is an *affiliate of each other at that time; and
(e) the issue of those shares is not an *acquisition of *ESS interests under an *employee share scheme; and
(f) immediately after that time, you do not hold more than 30% of the equity interests in the company or in an entity *connected with the company.

Members of trusts or partnerships

(2) A *member of a trust or partnership at the end of an income year is entitled to a *tax offset for the income year if the trust or partnership would be entitled to a tax offset, under subsection (1), for the income year if the trust or partnership were an individual.

Trustees

(3) A trustee of a trust is entitled to a *tax offset for an income year if:

(a) the trustee would be entitled to a tax offset, under subsection (1), for the income year if the trustee were an individual; and
(b) the trustee is liable to be assessed or has been assessed, and is liable to pay *tax, on a share of, or all or a part of, the trust's *net income under section 98, 99 or 99A of the *Income Tax Assessment Act 1936* for the income year.

360-20 Limited entitlement for certain kinds of investors

(1) You do not satisfy paragraph 360-15(1)(b) if:

(a) for each offer resulting in *equity interests that are *shares in the company being issued to you during the income year, none of subsections 708(8), (10) or (11) of the *Corporations Act 2001* removed the need for a disclosure document; and

(b) a total of more than $50,000 was paid for the issue to you of the shares resulting from all of those offers.

(2) For the purposes of this section, assume that Chapter 6D of the *Corporations Act 2001* applies to those offers.

360-25 Amount of the tax offset—general case

(1) If subsection 360-15(1) applies, the amount of the *tax offset is 20% of the total amount paid for the *shares to which paragraph 360-15(1)(b) applies.

Note: If subsection 360-15(1) applies for shares issued to you at several times during the income year, then this subsection uses the total amount paid for all of those shares.

(2) However, reduce this amount to the extent necessary to ensure that the sum of the following does not exceed $200,000:

(a) the sum of the *tax offsets under this Subdivision for the income year for which you and your *affiliates (if any) are entitled;

(b) the sum of the tax offsets under this Subdivision that you and your affiliates (if any) carry forward to the income year.

360-30 Amount of the tax offset—members of trusts or partnerships

(1) If subsection 360-15(2) applies, the amount of the *member's *tax offset for the income year is as follows:

Determined share of notional tax offset x Notional tax offset amount

where:

determined share of notional tax offset is the percentage determined under subsection (2) for the *member.

notional tax offset amount is what would, under section 360-25, have been the amount of the trust's or partnership's *tax offset (the ***notional tax offset***) if the trust or partnership had been an individual.

(2) The trustee or partnership may determine the percentage of the notional tax offset that is the *member's share of the notional tax offset.

(3) If the *member would be entitled to a fixed proportion of any *capital gain from a *disposal were the disposal to happen in relation to the trust or partnership at the end of the income year, then:

(a) the percentage determined under subsection (2) must be equivalent to that fixed proportion; and

(b) a determination of any other percentage has no effect.

(4) The trustee or partnership must give the *member written notice of the determination. The notice:

(a) must enable the member to work out the amount of the member's *tax offset by including enough information to enable the member to work out the member's share of the notional tax offset; and
(b) must be given to the member within 3 months after the end of the income year, or within such further time as the Commissioner allows.

(5) The sum of all the percentages determined under subsection (2) in relation to the *members of the trust or partnership must not exceed 100%.

360-35 Amount of the tax offset—trustees

If subsection 360-15(3) applies, the amount of the *tax offset is the difference between:

(a) what would, under section 360-25, have been the amount of the tax offset to which the trustee would have been entitled if the trustee had been an individual; and
(b) if *members of the trust are entitled to tax offsets under subsection 360-15(2) arising from the same *shares to which the trustee's entitlement arises under subsection 360-15(3)—the sum of the amounts, under section 360-30, of those tax offsets.

360-40 Early stage innovation companies

(1) This subsection applies to a company at a particular time (the ***test time***) in an income year (the ***current year***) if:

(a) the company was:

(i) incorporated in Australia within the last 3 income years (the latest being the current year); or
(ii) incorporated in Australia within the last 6 income years (the latest being the current year), and across the last 3 of those income years it and its *100% subsidiaries (if any) incurred total expenses of $1 million or less; or
(iii) registered in the *Australian Business Register within the last 3 income years (the latest being the current year); and

(b) the company and its 100% subsidiaries (if any) incurred total expenses of $1 million or less in the income year before the current year; and
(c) the company and its 100% subsidiaries (if any) had a total assessable income of $200,000 or less in the income year before the current year; and
(d) at the test time, none of the company's *equity interests are listed for quotation in the official list of any stock exchange in Australia or a foreign country; and

(e) at the test time, the company has at least 100 points under section 360-45, or:

(i) the company is genuinely focussed on developing for commercialisation one or more new, or significantly improved, products, processes, services or marketing or organisational methods; and
(ii) the business relating to those products, processes, services or methods has a high growth potential; and
(iii) the company can demonstrate that it has the potential to be able to successfully scale that business; and
(iv) the company can demonstrate that it has the potential to be able to address a broader than local market, including global markets, through that business; and
(v) the company can demonstrate that it has the potential to be able to have competitive advantages for that business.

(2) For the purposes of paragraph (1)(c), disregard any Accelerating Commercialisation Grant under the program administered by the Commonwealth known as the

(3) Subparagraphs (1)(e)(i) to (v) cannot be satisfied for:

(a) a product, process, service or method; or
(b) an improvement to a product, process, service or method;

that is of a kind prescribed by regulations made for the purposes of this subsection.

(4) Subsection (1) does not apply to a company if, before the test time, the company engaged in an activity of a kind prescribed by regulations made for the purposes of this subsection.

360-45 100 point innovation test

(1) At a particular time (the ***test time***) in an income year (the ***current year***), a company has the points mentioned in an item of the following table if that item applies to the company at that time.

Innovation points potentially available at that time in the current year		
	Column 1	Column 2
Item	Points	Innovation criteria
1	75	At least 50% of the company's total expenses for the previous income year is expenditure that the company can notionally deduct for that income year under section 355-205 (about R&D expenditure).
2	75	The company has received an Accelerating Commercialisation Grant under the program administered by the Commonwealth known as the Entrepreneurs' Programme.
3	50	At least 15%, but less than 50%, of the company's total expenses for the previous income year is expenditure that the company can notionally deduct for that income year under section 355-205 (about R&D expenditure).

Innovation points potentially available at that time in the current year		
	Column 1	Column 2
Item	Points	Innovation criteria
4	50	(a) the company has completed or is undertaking an accelerator program that: (i) provides time-limited support for entrepreneurs with start-up businesses; and (ii) is provided to entrepreneurs that are selected in an open, independent and competitive manner; and (b) the entity providing that program has been providing that, or other accelerator programs for entrepreneurs, for at least 6 months; and (c) such programs have been completed by at least one cohort of entrepreneurs.
5	50	(a) a total of at least $50,000 has been paid for *equity interests that are *shares in the company; and (b) the company issued those shares to one or more entities that: (i) were not *associates of the company immediately before the issue of those shares; and (ii) did not acquire those shares primarily to assist another entity become entitled to a *tax offset (or a modified CGT treatment) under this Subdivision; and (c) the company issued those shares at least one day before the test time.
6	50	(a) the company has rights (including equitable rights) under a *Commonwealth law as: (i) the patentee, or a licensee, of a standard patent; or (ii) the owner, or a licensee, of a plant breeder's right; granted in Australia within the last 5 years (ending at the test time); or (b) the company has equivalent rights under a *foreign law.
7	25	Unless item 6 applies to the company at the test time: (a) the company has rights (including equitable rights) under a *Commonwealth law as: (i) the patentee, or a licensee, of an innovation patent granted and certified in Australia; or (ii) the owner, or a licensee, of a registered design registered in Australia; within the last 5 years (ending at the test time); or (b) the company has equivalent rights under a *foreign law.
8	25	The company has a written agreement with: (a) an institution or body listed in Schedule 1 to the *Higher Education Funding Act 1988* (about institutions or bodies eligible for special research assistance); or (b) an entity registered under section 29A of the *Industry Research and Development Act 1986* (about research service providers); to co-develop and commercialise a new, or significantly improved, product, process, service or marketing or organisational method.

(2) At the test time, the company also has the points prescribed by regulations made for the purposes of this subsection if the prescribed innovation criteria for those points apply to the company at that time.

360-50 Modified CGT treatment

(1) This section applies if the issuing of a *share to an entity gives rise to an entitlement to a *tax offset under this Subdivision.

Note: This section applies to any share that gives rise to the entitlement, regardless of whether subsection 360-25(2) reduces the amount of the tax offset.

(2) The entity is taken to hold the *share on capital account.

(3) The entity must disregard any *capital loss it makes from any *CGT event happening in relation to the *share if:

(a) the entity has continuously held the share since its issue; and
(b) the CGT event happens before the tenth anniversary of the issue of the share.

(4) The entity may disregard any *capital gain it makes from any *CGT event happening in relation to the *share if:

(a) the entity has continuously held the share since its issue; and
(b) the CGT event happens on or after the first anniversary, but before the tenth anniversary, of the issue of the share.

(5) If the entity has continuously held the *share since its issue, the *first element of its *cost base and *reduced cost base becomes, on the tenth anniversary of its issue, its *market value on that anniversary.

360-55 Modified CGT treatment—partnerships

(1) The purpose of this section is to ensure that the modifications made by section 360-50 apply to each partner in a partnership in a case where the partnership is the entity that is issued with the *share mentioned in subsection 360-50(1).

(2) In such a case, subsections 360-50(2) to (4) apply as if:

(a) the first reference in those subsections to the entity were a reference to each partner in the partnership; and
(b) the first reference in those subsections to the *share were a reference to the partner's interest in the share.

Note: The references to the entity and the share in the paragraphs of subsections 360-50(3) and (4) continue to apply unchanged.

(3) In such a case, treat subsection 360-50(5) as if it read as follows:

"If the partnership has continuously held the *share since its issue, on the tenth anniversary of its issue:

(a) the *first element of the *cost base for a partner's interest in the share becomes so much of the share's *market value on that anniversary as is calculated by reference to the partnership agreement, or partnership law if there is no agreement; and
(b) the *first element of the *reduced cost base is worked out similarly.".

360-60 Modified CGT treatment—not affected by certain roll-overs

(1) The purpose of this section is to ensure that the modifications made by section 360-50 are not affected merely because of one or more *same-asset roll-overs or *replacement-asset roll-overs (other than roll-overs under Division 122 or Subdivision 124-M).

(2) If, apart from those roll-overs, the entity (the ***original entity***) mentioned in subsection 360-50(1) would continue to hold the *share (the ***original share***) mentioned in that subsection, then subsections 360-50(2) to (5) apply as if:

(a) the following asset were the original share:

(i) if the last roll-over is a *same-asset roll-over—the asset for the roll-over;

(ii) if the last roll-over is a *replacement-asset roll-over—the replacement asset for the roll-over; and

Note: The asset for subparagraph (i) will be the original share unless a replacement-asset roll-over happened beforehand.

(b) that asset was issued when the original share was issued; and

(c) the entity that *acquired that asset for the roll-over had continuously held that asset since the original share was issued; and

(d) that entity were the original entity; and

(e) in a case where that entity is a partnership—paragraphs (a) to (d) modify subsections 360-50(2) to (5) as they apply with the modifications in section 360-55; and

(f) in a case where that entity is not a partnership but the entity that owned the original asset for the roll-over is—paragraphs (a) to (d) modify subsections 360-50(2) to (5) as they apply without the modifications in section 360-55.

Note: A roll-over under Division 122 (about wholly-owned companies) or Subdivision 124-M (about scrip for scrip roll-overs) will stop the modified CGT treatment under section 360-50 from continuing to apply.

360-65 Separate modified CGT treatment for roll-overs about wholly-owned companies or scrip for scrip roll-overs

(1) If:

(a) a *share mentioned in subsection 360-50(1) has been continuously held by the entity mentioned in that subsection; and

(b) then:

(i) the share, or interests in the share, are *disposed of in a way that gives rise to a trigger event (see section 122-15 or 122-125) for a roll-over under Division 122; or

(ii) the share becomes the original interest (see paragraph 124-780(1)(a)) for a roll-over under Subdivision 124-M; and

(c) the roll-over happens on or after the first anniversary, but before the tenth anniversary, of the issue of the share;

the *first element of the *cost base and *reduced cost base of the share just before the roll-over is taken to be its *market value at that time.

Note: This subsection is a separate modified CGT treatment, and not a continuation of the modifications made by section 360-50.

(2) If:

(a) an asset mentioned in paragraph 360-60(2)(a) for a roll-over has been continuously held by the entity that *acquired that asset for that roll-over; and

(b) then:

(i) that asset, or interests in that asset, are *disposed of in a way that gives rise to a trigger event (see section 122-15 or 122-125) for a roll-over under Division 122; or

(ii) that asset becomes the original interest (see paragraph 124-780(1)(a)) for a roll-over under Subdivision 124-M; and

(c) the later roll-over happens on or after the first anniversary, but before the tenth anniversary, of the issue of the original share (see subsection 360-60(2) for the earlier roll-over;

the *first element of the *cost base and *reduced cost base of that asset just before the later roll-over is taken to be its *market value at that time.

Note: This subsection is a separate modified CGT treatment, and not a continuation of the modifications made by section 360-50.

Index

S. Barkoczy, T. Wilkinson, *Incentivising Angels*, SpringerBriefs in Law,
https://doi.org/10.1007/978-981-13-6632-1

S

T

V

The manufacturer's authorised representative in the EU is Springer Nature Customer Service Centre GmbH, Europaplatz 3, 69115 Heidelberg, Germany. If you have any concerns regarding our products, please contact ProductSafety@springernature.com

Printed and bound by CPI Group (UK) Ltd, Croydon, CR0 4YY

30/09/2026

02225468-0016